The Taliessin Poems
of Charles Williams

BY VARIOUS HANDS

EDITED BY ANNE RIDLER

*Published in cooperation
with the Charles Williams Society*

the apocryphile press
BERKELEY, CA
www.apocryphile.org

apocryphile press
BERKELEY, CA

Apocryphile Press
1700 Shattuck Ave #81
Berkeley, CA 94709
www.apocryphile.org

First published by the Charles Williams Society in 1991.
First Apocryphile edition, 2010.

For sale in the USA only. Sales prohibited in the UK.
Printed in the United States of America.

ISBN 978-1-933993-92-8

Other books by C.W. referred to:
Windows of Night (poems), Oxford 1924
Three Plays, Oxford 1931
Descent into Hell, Faber 1937
Arthurian Torso (Williams and Lewis), Oxford 1948

TABLE OF CONTENTS

Introductory Note   5

Taliessin through Logres
- Prelude   7
- Taliessin's Return to Logres   11
- The Vision of the Empire   13
- The Calling of Arthur   20
- Mount Badon   22
- The Crowning of Arthur   24
- Taliessin's Song of the Unicorn   28
- Bors to Elayne: The Fish of Broceliande   31
- Taliessin in the School of the Poets   34
- Taliessin on the Death of Virgil   37
- The Coming of Palomides   39
- Lamorack and the Queen Morgause   42
- Bors to Elayne: On the King's Coins   45
- The Star of Percivale   47
- The Ascent of the Spear   49
- The Sister of Percivale   50
- The Son of Lancelot   55
- Palomides before His Christening   61
- The Coming of Galahad   64
- The Departure of Merlin   68
- The Death of Palomides   70
- Percivale at Carbonek   72
- The Last Voyage   75
- Taliessin at Lancelot's Mass   78

The Region of the Summer Stars
- Prelude   80
- The Calling of Taliessin   83
- Taliessin in the Rose-Garden   87
- The Departure of Dindrane   93
- The Founding of the Company   95
- The Queen's Servant   98
- The Meditation of Mordred   100
- The Prayers of the Pope   102

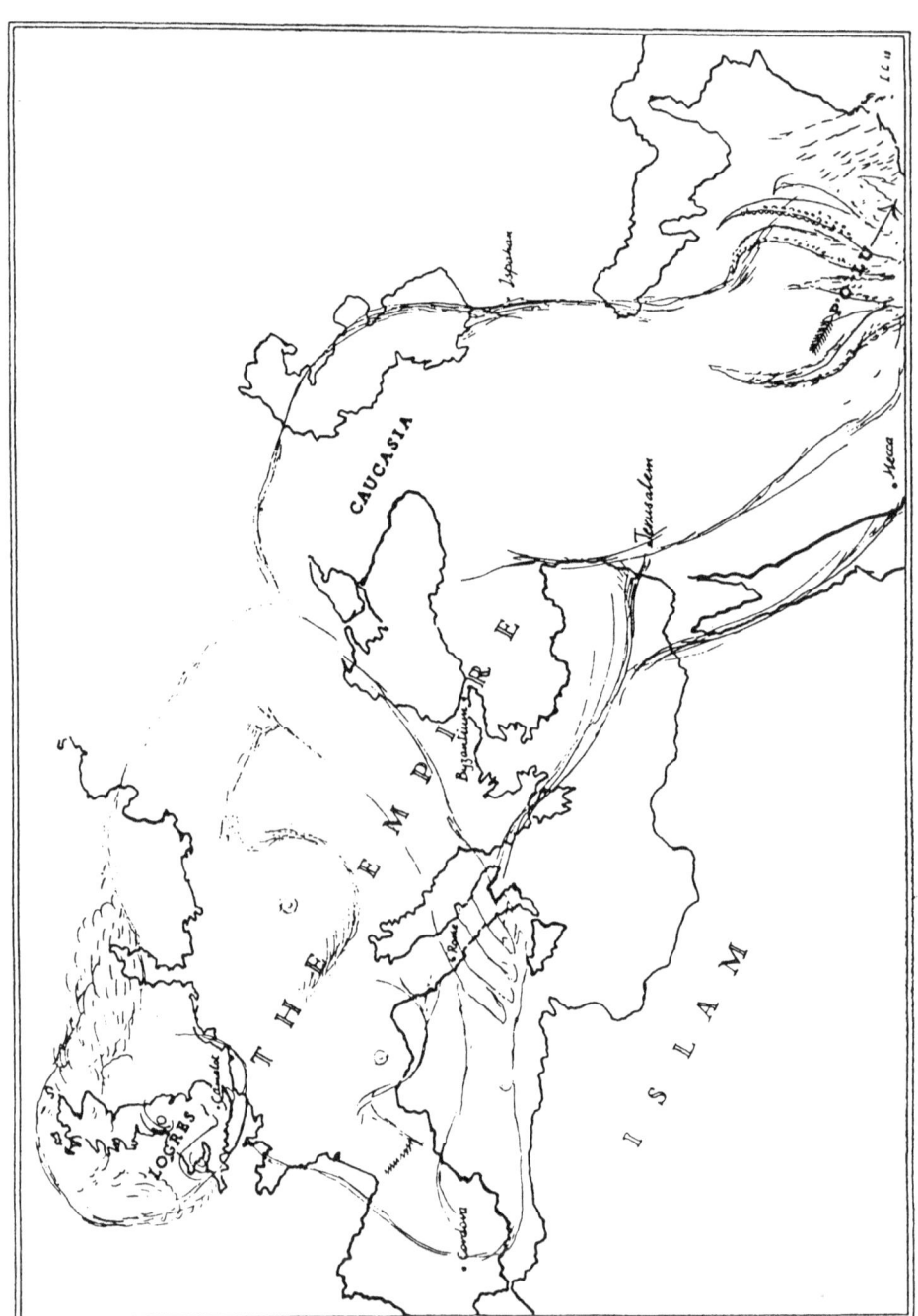

INTRODUCTORY NOTE

As a supplement to the quarterly Newsletter of the Charles Williams Society, some commentaries on his cycle of Arthurian poems were published between the years 1977 and 1986. The idea of writing these notes came from Alice Mary Hadfield: she allocated and to some extent monitored the contributions, which were sent in by half a dozen people who had had the benefit of C. W.'s own comments on the poems during the years when he was writing them.

Although Williams himself always refused to write a systematic exposition of his ideas, he did in fact leave a body of explanatory comments in different places: at the end of *Taliessin through Logres*; in the preface to the *Region of the Summer Stars*; and in two essays which were reprinted in the posthumous *Image of the City*. There exists also an invaluable typescript of some notes he wrote in answer to questions put to him by C. S. Lewis. Although the writers of the Newsletter notes used some of these in their commentaries, it seems best to reproduce a good many of them here, prefacing the poems concerned, for the benefit of other readers.

I have undertaken to edit and conflate the quarterly supplements, removing some of the inevitable repetitions, and clarifying some points further, in the hope that the notes will be more conveniently usable by students of the poems in this form. I offer it to the memory of Alice Mary Hadfield.

The writers of the supplements were Alice Mary Hadfield, Anne Ridler, Anne Scott, Thelma Shuttleworth, Joan and Richard Wallis. Their authorship is indicated by initials after the title of the relevant poem. As line-numbers were not printed with the text, readers will have to make their own calculations; the longer poems have been divided by paragraphs.

The original edition of *T. T. L.* had an endpaper map (drawn by Lynton Lamb) showing a woman's body superimposed on a map of the Empire: this is often referred to in the notes, and is reproduced

Introductory Note

here on the opposite page. Williams wrote of his general scheme (in the notes for Lewis) as follows:

> The Empire then is (a) all Creation – with logothetes and what not as angels and such (b) Unfallen (c) a proper social order (d) the true physical body. I left it female in appearance because the Emperor must be masculine, but this is accidental. The Empire is the pattern; Logres the experiment. The Emperor is (i) God-in-operation or God-as-known-by-man (ii) Fate (iii) operative force – as and according to the person concerned, but mostly here the God relation. Islam is (a) Theism (b) Manichaeanism (c) heavy morality (d) Islam. The themes are the divisions of the Empire – Caucasia, Gaul, Logres, etc. Caucasia is the physical fundamental – (a) the buttocks (b) basic senses (c) direct sex (d) village society. Gaul is 'fruitfulness' (a) the breasts (b) traditional organisation (c) scholastic debates and doctrines (d) theology. Byzantium is rather the whole concentration of body and soul than any special *member*. (The Lady Julian, I found last night, says that the City is built at the meeting-place of 'substance' and 'sensuality'.) The pirates are barbarous and chaotic instincts and uncivil ideas. The slaves are (I think) the pirates' kindred or captives or captives from the other themes (cf. Circassian girl in the *Arabian Nights*). Taliessin is the poetic imagination in this world and Percivale the imagination of the other and of the universe; he is the brother of Blanchefleur = substitution.
>
> The 'cut' hazel is measurement and power – of any kind, and the 'uncut' and the hazel-nuts are the fruit: it is the measure of doctrine in Lateran and the Church; of morality to the slaves, of 'psychology' to Merlin; it grows everywhere in Logres, and is at once the necessity of abstract statement, commands, and so on, as 'cut', and the actuality of 'natural grace' (so to call it) as 'uncut'.

A. R.

TALIESSIN THROUGH LOGRES

(Oxford, 1938)

Dedication

Humphrey Milford was publisher to the University of Oxford and head of the University Press London branch at Amen House, where C. W. worked as editor from 9 June 1908 to 4 September 1939, during which time these poems were written. Byzantium was from A. D. 330 the capital of the Eastern Roman Empire, and since C. 6 the Patriarch of Constantinople, as Byzantium was then called, was head of Eastern Orthodox Christianity. Logres (later Britain) is imaged as a member of the Empire, but of Western Christianity. C.W. chose the name and office of Byzantium as an image of a relationship of love exchanged between men in public, religious, working, or private life, and within man (as a little state) himself. A hierarchical order and wisdom develop an exchange of love, art, growth, and ability. (See notes on first poem.) Latin quotation from Dante's *De Monarchia*: 'Wherefore it is that the proper function does not come into existence for the sake of the being, but the latter for the sake of the former' (tr. Wicksteed, Hull, 1897).

PRELUDE

> The Empire of the poem exists as the substance of the actual Empire, and (like Logres) it half withdraws and half becomes history, because Logres has fallen, and our understanding has diminished . . . I add that the holy Empire does become continually visible, even in its theme of Caucasia; it renews itself to our sight. The fall of Logres has made everything difficult. But we can at least recognize the Empire – at Amen House or a score of other places – when we see it. Or we can feel the Emperor riding in the skies and see the flung stars – flashes of perception. It is at such moments that we begin again on the building up of Logres. (C. W.)

Prelude

Further notes by T. S.

Line 1. Natural man, man in disorder in himself and against others, chaotic instincts, uncivil ideas.

2. Religious, Christian, trinitarian wisdom, declaring the taking of manhood by Jesus the Son of God, and thereby the capacity of man to know and enter a full capacity of love.

Caucasia: province near centre of Empire; image of natural qualities of goodness and beauty in the body of man, of the civilised world and of Nature; also stable balance. These are interchangeable in the image, each being itself, the other, or all at once.

Thule: the farthest known point of the Empire, usually the Orkneys, but as completely part of it as Caucasia. In map of Empire overlaid by outline of woman's body, printed with first edition of the poems, Logres finds place in the skull, the focal point of nervous system and intelligence, and Byzantium at sympathetic nerve centre, Caucasia the buttocks.

4. Sophia: wisdom. As Dante began *The Divine Comedy* 'midway the path of life that men pursue' so Taliessin is in the condition when knowledge and experience combine in wisdom. He is ready now to write. The Arthurian period chosen for poems was midway between mystery and history.

5-6. Kingdom in Britain: related to the Emperor and wisdom. Wisdom relates to Christian myth of Incarnation of God-in-man; Arthurian myth is of man's struggle in mere 'necessity of being', exploiting rhythms, patterns, supernatural intimations in an effort with inherent qualities and circumstances to find place in general scheme, grow into it coherently, be in-Godded. Cathedral in Byzantium was dedicated to Holy Wisdom or Saint Sophia.

7. Carbonek: place, or state, of life in the spirit, of dedicated lives; here King Pelles watched over the Hallows.

Camelot: place, or state, of intelligence, of government, business, daily being and doing.

Caucasia: natural functions of delight, fertility, fruition.

Prelude

8. Gates: openings – eyes, ears, perceptions.
Containers: cities, buildings, skull, thorax, pelvis.
Intermediations: lucidity going between, interpreting.

9. Geography: natural shapes of earth's surface and the body.
Breathing geometry: (i) definition of shape and size 'for resemblance and communication' (*The Greater Trumps*) (ii) the mind; the two living by the Logos double-fledged as everything is two-in-one, itself coinhering with its opposite; here winged for swiftness.
Logos: the Word, which St. John says was in the beginning with God, was God. Now the poet has power, fitting stone (fact, experience) to shell (art, imagination – Wordsworth, *Prelude* V), knowing coinherence. All is most well.

10. But it is not. There are none so blind as those who won't see. Arthur later sees the kingdom as made for his ideas, for him, the King.

11. The fallacy of virtue thought out by man for useful results. Arthur organised might for right, but failed to inculcate right-mindedness.

12. Arthur rejected Papal Bull (with Pope's seal on it) forbidding him to go to war with Lancelot for love of the Queen. Round Table had united qualities and capacities in its knights represented here by its chairs. Now unity is broken, each man for himself or his group, chairs reeled.

13. Galahad: man's capacity for Christ, for salvation; G.'s following and achievement of Holy Grail shows further chance of redemption in God's mercy, a new start; G.'s conception was a working of substitution, when under enchantment Lancelot had intercourse with Elayne who loved him instead of with Guinevere whom he loved and to whom he was faithful.

Prelude

14. Byzantium captured by Islam which is an alien culture denying (a) that God became incarnate, (b) that godhead is in flesh and all matter, (c) a further chance of redemption, Fate will decide. The line is also an image of man's body or nature when undermined by shock or evil.

16. Hills carry image of Wordsworth's poetry, and fugitives from war or conscience; also of mind's dereliction (as Wentworth's, *Descent into Hell*), withdrawing into self-sufficiency, refusing courteous exchange inherent in City (heavenly, London-in-Logres, Rome, anywhere) imaged as container of all relationships where civil citizens choose to live, under government, each in his own way for all, all for God. Betrayal is from within as well as from an outer enemy, in refusing charity which allows us to be seen as no more than a flash of the Emperor's glory.

20. Ispahan: in map and sketch this is place of rejection (i) Moslem rejection of matter as holy (ii) body's ejection of waste through rectum. Before the Moslems, Zoroaster had taught that Good (Ormuz) and Evil (Ahriman) were twins but Ormuz would certainly conquer Ahriman.
    'Alla il Alla: God is one God'.

22-24. No joy or honour now in Caucasia. It is known only to be used or abused. Natural bounty is ravaged by toughs (mamelukes), and the religious leaders (imams) repudiate the Incarnation; dichotomy instead of union in man.

25. Good is God: but to Moslems God was never in-manned, so man cannot be in-Godded.

26-27. Innate goodness of the body proper to balance of whole man in love and life is lost; so too is recognition of the body to show the whole being and glimpses of creative light and glory.

TALIESSIN'S RETURN TO LOGRES (T.S.)

1-8. The poet home from Byzantium, a long apprenticeship ended, a man settling to his life, C. W. in Amen House.

9. Glory of Providence operating on his behalf seen above him 'in patines of bright gold' (*Merchant of Venice* V.i.).

11-15. Familiar, 7-starred Charles' Wain, or The Plough; mystical, Apocalyptical 7; magical, 7-pointed; poetical, 7 in Blessed Damosel's hair; all at-oned with golden sickle flashing 7 times in ceremonials in priestly-poetical rites of Druids; all in man's experience.

18-19. Harp, the poetic imagination, the feeling intellect, sounds the way which had been a blindfold track through darkness of great woods of literature. States of being he had found in Milton, Malory, Keats, Wordsworth, bring him now to his own forest, which includes theirs as theirs his.

22. Circe's son: Comus.

32. Flooding seas: cf. *Prelude* V.129.

33-36. He trusts to poetry, commits himself to be a poet, in the mercy of God.

37. Broceliande: a great wood with deep sea-inlets; place of making, making of man's mind and nature, of Nature itself, of all secrets of power; place of vast, awful, dangerous possibilities. It lies on SW coast of Logres. Carbonek is on seaward side, whence one can sail to Sarras in the Land of the Trinity (meaning affirmation of goodness), or further to P'o-Lu the negation of goodness, whose evil octopods are gripped by the roots of Broceliande's great trees penetrating the world even to Antipodean seas.

Taliessin's Return to Logres

38-40. He recognises a signal for himself, flash of sickle or golden arm which, (ll. 42-48) in midst of everyday things — masts, roads, farms — caught the Hallows (the witnesses of love in the Spear and Nails of Christ's Passion and the Grail or chalice He used at the Last Supper). He sees these as blessings: (l. 49) first, his falling in love; second, his rescue from terror of mind's overthrow; third, his arrival in settled job and place in the world.

52. Wood...worst: cf. *Inferno*, I.7.: 'Tanto è amara, che poco è piu morte'.

55-56. The password is poetry.

57-60. Druid light and King Arthur's horse: past and present, poetry and order coinhering.

THE VISION OF THE EMPIRE (A.R.)

α 1-4. The vision is Taliessin's.
Organic: in the meaning 'interconnected' as well as 'living'.
Dialects: variety of kinds, for men are as they speak. They issue from Byzantium as the place of creation, and return to it as the creation gives back its own image to God.
But for 'sound of the Throne', cf. the poem in *Windows of Night* (p. 76) on the lions behind Solomon's throne whose 'reiterant roar' confirms his judgements.

5-11. God is pure Act: a favourite definition from Thomas Aquinas. But the unity of the primal Act is dispersed ('abated') among phenomena, and the agents of this dispersal are the Emperor's household (inscribing, translating) and logothetes. We ourselves share in this activity, using and modifying in our own lives and loves the truths learnt in moments of vision.
Logothetes in C. W.'s usage is angel, messenger, though its original meaning was auditor, or Byzantine functionary.
Porphyry stair: All beginning efforts; not only a stair of porphyry, royal purple, but also recalling the porphyry chamber where, in Byzantium, the Empresses gave birth.

13. Exposition...images: from the interpreters to the diversity of the created world. C. W. wrote: 'He has gone out of the direct presence of the Emperor into the outer world, which is precisely a place of images; from the Sacred Palace to the waters of the Golden Horn, from "God in Himself" to "God in his creatures".' He has gone from the direct presence to the outer world, as men in love must do.

β 1-3. In the 'mirror of the Horn' Taliessin sees 'God in his creatures' with their separate identities.
Sinai: the first law and promise.
Ararat: The Ark and first act of salvation, God's pledge to man.
Elburz: (a late discovery in C. W.'s development of the myth): a high mountain in Caucasus (see 'Caucasia', below), which in the poem represents the true physical glory. C. W.: 'The grand type of

Vision of the Empire

the mingled lowness and height, fertility and chastity, verdure and snow, of the visible body'. C. W. had read that it was supposed to be the mountain where Prometheus, the fire-bringer, was chained.

5. Caucasia: In the cycle of poems, it was originally Circassia, derived from the Circassian girl in the Arabian Nights, till C. W. found that this would not hold the weight of meaning that he wished for it. Caucasia was 'more historic . . . was capable of *meaning* more' (*Image*, p. 181). He thought of it as 'direct sex' and 'village society', as well as the basic senses, and the buttocks in the diagram.

13 et seq. Dancing war: amorous strife; see *Heroes and Kings*, 'Lamorack's Song to Morgause', and elsewhere. The round mounds, the buttocks, are defending dales of fertility, yet are meant to be stormed. The maids (kindred to pirates, who are the instincts in chaotic shape) are microcosms of the Empire's shape, seen in its provinces.

The lost name: possibly because false shame is associated with Caucasia, so that the buttocks cannot be truly named.

20. The fool's shame: C. W. wrote (in 'The Making of Taliessin', *Image of the City*, p. 181): 'I can never see why the buttocks are funnier than any other part of the body; they support us when we sit, they are balance and (in that sense) justice. They are erotic, it is true, and that was an advantage for the poem; but they are plainly and naturally so; they are not mixed up, as eyes or hands may be, with the active moral question'.

γ 1 et seq. Taliessin, looking out at the images, sees Elburz reflected in the Golden Horn.

Theme: province (as in Gibbon); *in* the design, rather than *of*, I think.

Time's metre: C. W.: 'Merlin is Time (or Time is Merlin – I don't know which is safer) and the high prophetic Intelligence of the world "brooding on things to come".' He is also definition and measurement.

Through prisms: as spatial measurement (Brisen) is the other

Vision of the Empire

half of his existence.

Percivale's philosophical star: Percivale is the supernatural imagination; phosphor, the morning star, is Venus when seen before sunrise – i.e. perhaps intellectual, unerotic love. Percivale is moved by reason – he refrained from asking the Question about the Grail (see *Torso*, p. 64 seq.). There is also his love for Blanchefleur/Dindrane, his 'sister', to be dealt with later.

Blazons of the brain: intellectual heraldry of the Table.

Plotted arms of the soul: cf. *Divorce*, 'House-hunting': 'The plotted comprehension of all souls'.

White nuntius: the Emperor's messenger.

δ 1 et seq. Breasts of Gaul: see notes to 'Prelude'. And: 'Gaul is "fruitfulness" . . . traditional organisation, scholastic debates and doctrines, and theology' (C. W.).

Trigonometrical milk: trinitarian, divine ('It is not good for God to be alone', an epigram often quoted by C. W.).

Breasts: the twin functions of thought and belief; cf. Anselm's *'Credo ut intelligam'*.

Taliessin grew from primitive Druid wisdom to Christian doctrine. In the first cycle of poems, he had gone to Byzantium with a plea to the Emperor for help in the wars of Logres. He brings his knowledge of poetry, the grand art, to Logres, helping to make it reflect a true aspect of Byzantium.

Aspect: as appearance in the Dedication to the book.

ε 1 et seq. Old sun: i.e. pre-history.

Morals: the structure of the body.

Cones: C. W.: 'The delicate and sensitive palms are conceived as full of points from which cones flow down into the *substance* of our being. The mass of the points makes up the activities and passivities of the hands, for which Rome stands, which is an image of Byzantium as the hands of the whole being'.

Finger-nails are the plough, and amorous sowing, and then the actual nails of the Cross, 'finishing the toil' for man.

The 'circle' is Christ, and the 'seed-springing surrender' is his Passion. The incantation of the Mass (also of pre-Christian priests)

Vision of the Empire

is changed to hands of adoration at the foot of the Cross.

Pointing: of the Psalms, and as pointing to the Mystery.

16-17. Flash of identity: when the Being of God is made known and Man is at one with it; manual acts in the celebration of the Mass, breaking Christ's body, and breaking man's heart for pity and gratitude.

ζ 1 et seq. A prelude to the Fall which is described in the next section. Marches, because redemption has to be at the distant parts of Empire.

Golden palaces pale to the Papal vesture: opulent gold gives way to ascetic white, in the priestly act of reparation for the Fall.

η 1 et seq. The Adam: collective singular for Adam and Eve before the Fall.

Jerusalem: the groin, area of the sexual organs which, according to Jewish tradition, were involved in the Fall. The Fall and the Crucifixion which redeemed it are located in the same geographical place — see the end-paper map, now available separately.

Twined: suggesting the serpent, the 'forked friend'.

Describing the Fall in *He Came down from Heaven*, chapter 2, C.W. called it 'an alteration in knowledge':

> The Adam had been created and were existing in a state of knowledge of good and nothing but good. They knew that there was some kind of alternative, and they knew that the rejection of the alternative was part of their relation to the Omnipotence that created them...But they knew also that the knowledge in the Omnipotence was greater than their own: they understood that in some way it knew 'evil'. (p. 17)

And they desired to share that knowledge:

> Man desired to know schism in the universe. It was a knowledge reserved to God; man had been warned that he could not bare it — 'in the day that thou eatest thereof thou shalt surely die'. A serpentine subtlety overwhelmed that statement with a grander promise — 'Ye shall be as gods, knowing good and evil'. Unfortunately to be as gods meant, for the Adam, to die,

Vision of the Empire

for to know evil, for them, was to know it not by pure intelligence (as God does) but by experience. It was, precisely, to experience the opposite of good, the slow destruction of the good, and of themselves with the good. (p. 18)
Thus they knew good *as* evil.

9-20. Climbing the tree of the knowledge of good and evil is the equivalent (I take it) of eating its fruit. And thus the Adam introduce the experience of division into the heart of the Empire. As they hang crucified, their double entity, their two bodies, good in themselves, lust against each other. They are forced to observe the Emperor's vision of the wars within identity, where all good is known as its opposite.

22. 'Without' here means 'outside', I think.

24. The Fall, the 'rejection of salvation' is as it were vomited out to the other part of the divided self. (I offer this as a possible explanation of an obscure line). The Adam see this without power to change it. Possibly (A. M. H. suggests) the 'white pulsing shape' is the semen, the sexual centre of life undirected by love or reason.

θ 1. Elburz, the true physical glory, sinks through the waters to P'o-lu, the extreme opposite of Byzantium, where the good of the universe is seen in reversal, the 'feet of creation walk backward'. The becalming of the ship recalls the *Ancient Mariner* to me, but I do not know if C. W. so intended.

7. Unaccumulated: unpleasant perhaps because not defined, as it would be if 'accumulated' in a visible mass. Definition and measurement are always characteristic of heaven in the poems.

8-12. Gold of Asia, carried over sea to be worked in Byzantium, another type of physical glory, is dulled. 'The galley seems like the gold-mine afloat, but all spoiled' (C. W.).

14-15. Cf. the doves (become sea-travellers) of the *Last Voyage*, A.M.H. suggests.

Vision of the Empire

18-22. The 'headless figure' is how the Emperor appears in P'o-lu. The image was taken from the tale recorded in Gibbon's *Decline and Fall of the Roman Empire,* of the vision of a monk who saw an ape seated on the Emperor Justinian's throne. 'Everything there is parodied, and holy intellect is lost', as C. W.'s note has it, and 'P'o-lu is the Chinese name, of about the period, for the point of Java — the extreme point (nobody knew New Zealand then)'.

Indecent hands: in self-absorbed masturbation? Not the controlling hands of l. 34.

23. The Emperor's guard are here seen as octopuses (C. W.'s chosen image for Hell developed in *The House of the Octopus*); their tentacles reach right to heaven, and two in attendance hold up the Emperor's cope, parodying the usual ceremonial.

The floor seems perpetually to sink away — an image of horror to be found in earlier work, notably the poem called 'Tartarus' (*Windows of Night*):
> Yet deep within me, wherever I stand or go,
> I feel now the suction, the drag, the desire of the void
> To swallow for ever the spirits of men . . .

28 et seq. '"Penis" — the headless Emperor's: why? because all capacities are reduced to a kind of sensational preoccupation with one thing, and that is why the crimson cope obscenely resembles the first high flush of Caucasian love. If one gets fixed on Caucasia — !' (C. W.'s Notes).

All intellectual experience is in a turmoil, uncertain in focus, a kaleidoscope, deprived of the defining power of speech. The 'Roman hands', the controlling hands of the Church, are powerless here: hands in general are enablers, reducing horror and chaos.

41 et seq. After the Fall, the redemption. The poem ends in a rapturous Benedicite, identity no longer divided within itself, the holy and glorious body in all its aspects, all its geographical points, adoring its Lord.

12. The Lateran palace on the Caelian hill in Rome came to the Church through Constantine's wife Fausta, and was the official residence of the Popes from the 4th Century till the Avignon separation. It was traditionally the site of Constantine's baptism, and the basilica is still the cathedral church of Rome ('omnium urbis et orbis ecclesiarum mater et caput'). In C. W.'s verse Lateran is the fount of Roman doctrine, the hill 'whence shining thoughts have come On Augustinian errand all the Saxon thanes must con' ('A Song of the Myths' in *Three Plays*).

THE CALLING OF ARTHUR (J.W.)

1. Arthur was young: an incident early in the story, when Arthur's life was still to be made. Merlin, among many meanings, is a wizard, and is also Time. He meets Arthur here at the moment of Arthur's destiny to lead the fight to free his country Logres from the pagan tyrants, and to rebuild the city of Camelot.

6. Camelot: the city was ruined under King Cradlemas, and Arthur is called to rebuild it and restore the centre of government and order in daily life. 'O Joan, O Anthea, O daughter of Camelot,' '..at least if we are building the City, we will, so far, build it' (letter from C.W. to Joan 1/vi/43 and undated letter of the war years).

7-8. Malory says Arthur fought 11 kings to gain his throne. In the poem the King of London, Cradlemas, is shown as a feeble remnant of Roman civilisation. Like Nero, he has an emerald for a monocle. 'The name was meant for Cradlement; that was a pure slip' (C.W.'s note).

12. The bleak mask is gilded: like the golden Mask of Agamemnon, though probably not Charles's intention.

25-28. Draw now...swing now: this is the time, the moment for a leader in action, hence Merlin meets Arthur.

27. Hammer and sickle: emblems of the labouring poor, and of particular political significance to the 20th Century.

28. Bors, the ordinary fellow, nephew of Lancelot, husband of Elayne, father of two children, a responsible man.

32. Lancelot, called 'of Gaul' or 'Du Lac', Arthur's chief friend and second-in-command.

33. O wave of Pendragon: the family name of Arthur used here, not his heraldic dragon but a rolling banner taken into battle like a wave to engulf the fragile sea-snail King Cradlemas.

The Calling of Arthur

34. O'ergilded: likely to be a pun by C. W. on the heraldic word *or* for gold.

37-39. Arthur answers the call, raises forces, defeats King Cradlemas.
Time (Merlin) brings return of peace and order, rebuilding of the central city in Logres and in man. 'The lyric ends in a fierce, glad rush of music as the builders, the food-bearers, the saviours overwhelm Cradlemas like a tide' ('Williams and the Arthuriad', C.S. Lewis).

MOUNT BADON (J.W.)

Title: The battle of Mons Badonicus, in which King Arthur finally defeated the invaders. An entry in *Annales Cambriae* quoted by Charles in 'The Figure of Arthur' (p. 8) reads '518. The battle of Badon in which Arthur carried the cross of our Lord Jesus Christ, for three days and three nights, on his shoulders, and the Britons were the victors'. Site of battle unknown, somewhere in the S. W. of England, where there are many earthworks.

In the poem the battle also suggests every man's turning point, some decision which affects his whole life.

1. The king's poet: Taliessin was also 'his captain of horse in the wars'. Taliessin is to be the poetic imagination of the king's Household, as the poet is vital to thought, and therefore, action. Throughout the poems Taliessin is a major figure; Charles's version of the myth is 'Taliessin through Logres'; he is courtier and recorder as well as a poet and cavalry leader.

4. The Dragon was Arthur's banner, the centre of his troops, his action.

5. Gawaine was son of Arthur's sister Morgause the Queen of Orkney, a strong knight.

7. Indiscriminate host: undisciplined, inaccurate.

11. Pirates are sea-robbers who invaded Britain after the withdrawal of the Roman legions, but Charles uses the word as 'chaotic instincts' (see his Notes). 'Nor did we bring you to this pitch of style to have it (saving God and the Emperor) interfered with by the pirates' (war-time letter from C. W. to Joan 13/ix/40).

24-40. In Taliessin's study of the battle, a parallel moment in Virgil arose in his mind; Virgil, poet and leader and founder of the City of Rome, stands on a 'trellised path by the sea' (l. 32). I suppose 'trellis' is to describe the growing of vines in the locality, the pastoral retreat of the poet, which is to be what Logres will become

Mount Badon

after Arthur's victory.

36. Charles's concern with the concept of the city. Virgil had defined Rome, had led Dante in Dante's poem *The Divine Comedy*, and Taliessin/Charles would be concerned with the foundation and definition of London and of the good life in man and between men.

Invention: indicates both finding and making. Charles wrote that Virgil 'imagined a moral world' ('Vergil' review in *Time and Tide* 1944 of a book by W. Jackson Knight).

42. Flash of his style: a small rod for writing on wax.

48. The tip of the spear resembles a style, the union of the captain and the writer.

50. I suppose the 'Aeneid's beaked lines' are the Roman galleys' prows in the Battle of Actium. Virgil's poem *The Aeneid* has even been held to be a disguised attack on Augustus ('Vergil' review). Is this the defeat of Anthony and the re-establishing of Rome by Augustus in Taliessin's vision?

55-62. For all this passage read also *The Revelation of St. John the Divine*, ch. I, vv. 12 onwards, and ch. XXI, v. 1 and vv. 15-27, for origins of the imagery.

55. Solstice: the mid-point of either winter or summer. The pagan festival of the winter solstice will be submerged into the Christian festival of Christmas.

56-57. Charles wrote 'The Maid-Mother's son was the foundation of all Cities' ('Vergil' review).

Arthur carries the Cross before him in battle. Another version is that he 'carried on his shoulders an image of St. Mary Ever-Virgin, and on that day the pagans were put to flight' ('Figure of Arthur' by C. W., pp. 6-7). Also, from the same book, '...and his shield Pridwen, on which was engraved in tracings of reddish gold the image of the blessed and glorious Mary' (p. 41).

THE CROWNING OF ARTHUR (A.M.H.)

This poem follows closely the theme of the Dante quotation at the beginning of the book.

1. King stood crowned: man or woman who has achieved whatever he needs to begin, to live well (job, marriage, vocation, etc.).

2. Midnight: turn from one day (the beginning) to the next, and so on.

8. Candles: their association with Christian worship and with orderly life contrasted with torches, associated with companies out of doors, crowds, etc.

9. Beasts of the banners: heraldic emblems of the knights; see note on 'Mount Badon', l. 4.

11. King's friend: Sir Lancelot.

11-25. Lancelot's lion: the beast on his shield. These four lines present Sir Lancelot's total devotion to the King. It is hard to find literary sources for the heraldic devices which follow. Many are probably the writer's own idea, as with earlier accounts. Tennyson, in 'Lancelot and Elaine', writes:
  'Sir Lancelot's azure lions crown'd with gold
  Ramp in the field'.

16. A closer definition of Merlin than just 'Time'.

17. Stephen: the cathedral in Camelot was dedicated to St. Stephen.

19-20. Sophia: double meaning (i) wisdom (ii) church of St. Sophia in Byzantium. Space, process, and the dark abysm of time are present in Merlin's vision. He sees that Arthur now has his moment (as everyone has) when scope, ability, and recognition come together for him.

The Crowning of Arthur

21-23. Merlin looks at the emblems on the shields of the knights through whom the King will have to build up and govern the kingdom.

24-51. Heraldic devices show a man's family, personality or achievements; they also indicate that as a knight he held a position under the King.

24-27. Azure: blue.
   Sidereally pointed: marked with stars.
   Fess of argent: fess is term for a band enclosed between two straight lines across the middle of the space.
   Argent: silver.

28. Queen Morgause (see Malory) was wife to King Lot of Orkney, mother of Gawaine and all his brothers; also sister to King Arthur 'on his mother's side' as no one knew who his father was.

30. Morgause had a love affair with Sir Lamorack son of King Pellinore, for which her sons killed Sir Lamorack.
   Sable: black.

31-35. The colours (tincture: the background colour of a shield) change to a silver dolphin (traditionally a sign of fair weather) on a crimson background, or, in bloody water.
   Naiant: swimming. Dinadan did not take too seriously either good circumstances (mockery) or being important (mockery); he regarded bad or good fortune equally cheerfully; a favourite character and image with C. W.

36-40. A pelican is supposed to peck blood from its breast to feed its young in hard times; often a symbol of Christian love. Sir Bors had one on his shield.
   To itself most fell: damaging itself most.

41-45. Besides the heraldic beasts devised by man, Merlin sees the forms and feelings of instinct and being rise from Broceliande, and the fish of Nimue its warden; each in its proper order, each equal before God, glory of Logres, and all making their patterns of the knowledge of Christ in the light of their day.

46-49. Taliessin (not a knight though cavalry leader and poet), from the crowd's, not Merlin's, angle of view, saw the heraldic emblems differently, as wildness formalised but not converted (C.W. said the poet would be accurate). This changes the suggestion of each man's character and contribution.

50. Romance and beauty enter the new life.

56. Lancelot moved: the first human action of the new reign in the poem.

57-61. Lancelot was the King's chief friend and executive of his will and ideas. So, here he led Guinevere to the King.
 The lions in the Byzantine glory: C. W. often spoke of the lions that stood on the steps of King Solomon's throne and roared when the King gave judgement. See sonnet in *Windows of Night*, p. 76.

62-63. The hinge of the poem – not the appearance of Guinevere, but the moral choice by a man whether to serve his function or to use his function as made for him.

64. Merlin had called Arthur to a life of service, rebuilding the city and the country (see 'The Calling of Arthur'). Or would he regard the power and office as being for his personal benefit?

65. The dolorous blow was the using of a sacred weapon for a man's personal benefit. It caused failure and wretchedness throughout the land until the coming of Galahad. C.W. felt this as a continuing possibility in people's lives.

66-69. Doom: future events.
 Shocks: colours changing strongly in torch light, and, also, surprises in future. C. W. liked this verse.

70. Taliessin had a thought of how all their effort might go wrong,

The Crowning of Arthur

all their thought of goodness might die.

71. I think the door of the gloom is the opening to the tomb in line 70.

73-75. First watch: first division of hours after midnight at sea and in the life of prayer; commonly felt to be lowest ebb of vitality. Matins was originally the first office of prayer after midnight.

74. C. W. said he had learnt that the call to prayer is in some Moslem mosques beaten on a hollow wooden board (or drum) and that (l. 75) some sects held that souls awaiting judgement cluster on a ledge over an abyss. At the hollow sound they shudder, both bad and good, at the approach of the spiritual life.

TALIESSIN'S SONG OF THE UNICORN

C. W.'s Note:
> Not very good. It had originally the notion that most women prefer direct attention to indirect labour; 'the unicorn' (poetry, social things, etc.) is regarded as less attractive than the human fellow; Catullus was a kind of 'catch' for Lesbia, but she much preferred less poetry and more intercourse, so she took up with someone else. On the other hand it is the great ideas by devotion to which we get things done. If a woman could really help poetry, poetry might say something. (Cf. the 'twy-nature' in 'Bors to Elayne') And so with all, including the B.V.M.

Further notes by A.M.H.

I remember (as others may) C.W. working on the later drafts of this poem, walking up and down his little office (4 paces each way) saying lines softly aloud, cigarette smoke drifting up past his specs. He would say, 'It's not good, it's not good'. Then go into various lines, mutter alterations and reject them. He never 'explained' a phrase.

1-2. See 'shouldering shapes' in 'The Crowning of Arthur' l. 41 and note. Instincts are from the making of nature and the taking of man's flesh by the Creator; can be flashes of insight into beauty's depth, into ability, glory, and spirit in the flesh, particularly in 'Caucasia', or, the body in native freedom and order.

4-5. Of the fabulous beasts the unicorn is the lordliest crest (heraldic) for verse.

7. Clear flesh: virgin.

6-15. A young woman may attract the unicorn, but then not want a love so different (alien) from herself and her experience, expressing an energy (snorting, galloped) and a new range of views and ideas (dusky horizon) it cannot explain; nor the display of power (silver horn pirouetting above her bosom) which is a threat to her ideas and offers no way to sexual satisfaction; her body is chilled and repelled, the organ of power made her shudder (gruesome), only something to be ministered to, 'polished, its rifling rubbed between breasts'.

16-19. She wants sexual play and pleasure and fulfillment, without a lot of intellectual/religious attention and interpretation, and certainly no sublimation.

19. C. W. thought much on Catullus, his poetic genius, his passion, tenderness, hate, and satire for Lesbia, and the suffering she willingly inflicted on him.
 Cuckold of the wood: the unicorn when the young woman had escaped from him.

20. West from Caucasia: not truly Caucasia whose women might have other development.

21. Yet there could be a way of uniting these two worlds of love, by a woman who was capable (having the cunning) of attracting a poet (grand beast: C. W. called poetry the grand art).

22. The animal which is but a shade till it starts to run: C. W. felt the poet is only known when he writes, or, in his writings. C. W.'s poetic criticism is grounded in this view.

23. From this line onwards I think there is possibly a double meaning:

24-28. i: The young woman should dare to hold the horn firmly, embrace the strange experience more and more deeply and accept a change in herself and in her whole nature. (The horizon would be less dusky as she approached it.) The horn might become a symbol of the lance piercing the body of Christ on the cross, so that her body's arteries or life held a new quality of rarity like crystal as well as blood. By embracing the way of love which was not known or familiar (dark bark) she would be able to transmute any experience until her whole life and the world round her (the wood)

Taliessin's Song of the Unicorn

turn into one knowledge or experience (one giant tree) through which she could gloriously live.

32-34. i: She would produce (her son) a new way of life and of poetry – the unicorn has no voice in l. 10 – which takes in the scope of the City of coinherence, substitution, and exchange, and also the old familiar instincts (enskied shouldering shapes); and in this new life the new knowledge of City and of instincts would be shown and known (each science disposed).

23-32. ii: Another possible meaning in lines 23-32. The horn would be the penis. If a woman dared to enter into the experience of combining love, sex, and poetry, she might join in both sexual exploration and attention to poetry little by little, ever increasing both in depth and commitment without dissipating or blurring by release into the act of sexual orgasm. Energy, imagination, and love would be concentrated in this development, the wood of the world become one giant tree, and her hands on the penis could carry the strength of the longing to each heart.

30, 32. 'Translucent, planted with virtues, lit by throes' could be a literal description of such love and life. From it would grow (her son) poetry with a new reach and penetration such as C. W. felt the genius of great poets was seeking. Again the unicorn: has no voice, l. 10, and l. 31, it has, 'a new sound'. This meaning could relate to the *subintroductae* of the early church who may have attempted something of the same concentration of energy with sex and religion. C. W. refers to this attempt in *Descent of the Dove*, ch. 1.

36. Paramour: C. W. insisted that the old meaning 'by or through love', or 'love' or 'lover' was wider than its modern 'illicit' gloss, and also that 'spouse' or 'husband' were not possible.

Intellectual nuptials unclosed: full attention and developing comprehension of each other's thoughts, imagination and ability.

Unclosed: not completed, ended or limited, but ever fresh, ever new.

BORS TO ELAYNE: THE FISH OF BROCIELIANDE

C. W.'s Note:
    Broceliande is somewhere round Cornwall and Devon, to the west of Logres. It is regarded both as a forest and as a sea – a sea-wood; in this sense it joins the sea of the antipodes which lies among its roots. Carbonek is beyond it: or at least beyond a certain part of it; C. stands between B. and the full open sea, beyond which is Sarras.
    Mystically it is the 'making' of things. Nimue is the Nature of Creation as the mother of Merlin (Time) and Brisen (Space): she is the source of movement and of distance. She is almost the same state represented by the Emperor's Court, but more vast, dim, and aboriginal. The huge shapes emerge from Broceliande, and the whole matter of the form of the Empire, and all this is felt in the beloved.
    I think the Fish is the strange quality in Romantic Love which comes from Broceliande originally and seems to flash through the beloved; here the beloved's body is seen so and not as the Empire. The Fish is not exactly Christ, but the early Church symbolised Christ by a Fish; so the light of Romantic Love is of Christ. It is something which perhaps could be found by two lovers, though it never is. Caucasia (or sense) is in a way as deep as Broceliande, and the divine *anthropos* is there. Bors offers what he receives; and he is the 'married man'.
    The twy-nature = two lovers (and, more extremely, Christ).

Further notes by A. S.

1. The king is building Camelot: after the triumph and the crowning, everyday life is to be made civilised and secure.

6. Define: map, explore the bounds of, as Lamorack does northwards in 'Lamorack and the Queen Morgause of Orkney'.
    Broceliande: see 'Taliessin's Return to Logres', l. 37. C. S. Lewis, in 'Williams and the Arthuriad' (p. 99), quotes a note by C.W. on Broceliande which ends 'From it the huge shapes emerge, the whole *matter* of the *form* of Byzantium – and all this is felt in

Bors to Elayne: The Fish of Broceliande

the beloved'.

13. C. W. once said that when confronted with a choice of apparently mutually exclusive alternatives – an either/or situation – the best response was often 'Neither: both!'; both alternatives were to be seized or followed or experienced with the utmost intensity to their uttermost conclusions. For the rest of the poem Bors is doing this. Elayne is at once his wife *and* a stream that flows through the forest that is Broceliande to the sea that is Broceliande. He looks at her hand, her arm, her shoulder with the passionate attention of all C. W.'s lovers, and that passionate attention sees them as a pool, a channel, a boulder in that stream. The fish is her gift to him *and* his gift to her and yet cannot be summoned or possessed by either of them.

17. How lordly at home is set the dish: a reminiscence of the Authorized Version of *Judges* V.25: 'She brought forth butter in a lordly dish'.

30. A twy-nature: Christ, 'The twy-natured single Person' (*Region of the Summer Stars*, 'Prelude', l. 51).

32. And if – inhumanly flashing a sudden scale: and even if it were to obey the summons it would come in all the strangeness of its own nature, not amenable to merely human ideas or desires.

37-38. Where the Catacomb's stone holds its diagram over the happy dead: during the early centuries of the persecution of the Church the outline of a fish was used as a symbol of Christ, because the Greek word for 'fish' was 'ICHTHUS' and those letters formed the initials of the title IESUS CHRISTOS THEOU-UIOS SOTER, Jesus Christ Son of God Saviour. Consequently the fish's outline would appear on the tombstones of many of the martyrs who were buried in the Catacombs.

43-48. The poem ends with the recognition of two more apparently opposing truths. Civilisation and order have really been achieved *and* the untameable forces of Broceliande 'probe through' every

Bors to Elayne: The Fish of Broceliande

intellectual or material pattern.

48. Substantial: actually existing, not illusory; of real importance or value. (*Concise Oxford Dictionary*)

TALIESSIN IN THE SCHOOL OF THE POETS

C. W.'s Note:
>Taliessin says that the light beginnings of measurement and understanding are easy enough. 'The creamed with crimson sphere' is the body; the centre line of which is given, obviously, and never is quite given: what we have is never quite right. The body may be measured (actually or morally or poetically); love may prick the coat of grace, but they best understand the living beauty of love who know the ascent in the Sacred Palace, the stair that leads to God (as the Emperor). The newel – the C. O. D. gives 'post supporting handrail of stair at top or bottom', so there could be two. The Throne is the place of eternity; every moment is equally the centre; and our impulses are themselves holy. To love is to merit; to see is to see rightly. It is the place of principles and of things as they are. The identity of love (for example) differs in the categories of sex, of the City, of religion. In the Throne is the identity; in the themes are the categories; in Logres is temporal understanding. In Logres therefore are the distances and the measurements and the need of precision.

Further notes by A. S.

2. Amen House was almost in the shadow of St. Paul's Cathedral, which C. W. here transfers to Camelot, which is London-in-Logres.

7. Phoebus Apollo was the god both of the sun and of poetry.

8. The Python was a serpent produced by the slime left by the Flood and slain by Apollo at Delphi.

27. Taliessin's speech is in praise of accuracy, precision, exactness. 'The word glory, to English ears, usually means no more than a kind of mazy bright blur. But the maze should be, though it generally is not, exact, and the brightness should be that of a geometrical pattern' (*He Came Down from Heaven*, Ch. III).

31. C. W.'s note on 'the creamed-with-crimson sphere' explains it

Taliessin in the School of Poets

as 'the human body, of which the centre line is given, obviously, and yet never quite given'. When I confessed to him that I could not help picturing this verse in terms of someone winding wool from a ball onto two crossed pipe-cleaners to make a doll he was much amused and said that it was a feminine version which had not occurred to him, but which had its points of resemblance.

37. For 'the measuring hazel rod' see the C. W.'s Note, quoted in the Introductory Note (p. iv).

42. 'Fly the porphyry stair' is analogous to 'walk the road' NOT to 'flee the stricken field'.

49. 'Indulged' in the sense of privileged, favoured.

52. 'Compensations' in the sense of counter-balances.

55 et seq. In Byzantium as an earthly type of the heavenly City everything can be seen to have its own unique importance: there every impulse is a response to divine grace, every movement of wonder at the glory a will to explore it, every impetus of love meritorious, and to see the goal is to advance towards it.

60. The Pandects: the complete body of laws.

68. For Virgil's place in C. W.'s 'mythology' see note on 'Mount Badon', ll. 24-40. See also 'Taliessin on the Death of Virgil', 'The Son of Lancelot', l. 50, 'The Last Voyage', ll. 14-17, the review 'Vergil', reprinted in *The Image of the City and Other Essays* and *The Figure of Beatrice*.

69. Taliessin, like C. W., is always conscious of the suffering in human lives, as well as of their glimpses of glory. Here he remembers Palinurus, the steersman of Aeneas and his companion in all his hardships and wanderings, who was thrown overboard by a god before they reached their longed-for goal of Italy and saw it only from the crest of a wave before he died.

Taliessin in the School of Poets

85-89. 'Tendebantque manus ripae ulterioris amore' (*Aeneid* VI.314) the ghosts of the unburied dead 'stretched out their hands in longing for the further shore' which they were unable to reach. As the young poets study the picture of the macrocosm enmeshed by the beams of Phoebus they hear 'the universal sigh' of all unsatisfied longings.

91-96. The 'patterns of multilinear red' have become in 'the sovereign chair's mass' as infinite as the expressions of poetry itself, but in 'the brass of a man' (l. 16) which the young poets have been studying, the patterns show the precision of 'bones, nerves, sinews' which make up 'the diagram of the style (in the sense of 'descriptive formula, designation of person, full title') of the Logos'. The Logos is the Second Person of the Blessed Trinity: his 'style' after the Incarnation is God-made-man. Also 'style' = pen.

101. Sis salvator, Domine: 'Be Thou a Saviour, O Lord'. A universally-known medieval prayer was 'Jesu, Jesu, esto mihi Jesus' – 'O Jesus, Jesus, be Jesus to me', because, as the Christian church teaches 'The holy name 'Jesus' means 'Saviour'.'

TALIESSIN ON THE DEATH OF VIRGIL

C. W.'s Note:
   It does not depend on his not knowing Christianity; we live, now and hereafter, by others, and the poem would apply equally to Dante. 'Augustus's buttocks' are the experience of good things – friendship, Rome – as horrible and obscene. The good really does *seem* revolting to us. Cf. the headless Emperor's penis in sex and love. ? a kind of dark night of the soul.

Further notes by T. S.

Charles wrote in a letter, c. 1934,
   ...there is a tale that even the Lord John Milton was saved after death by the myriad wings of his lovers who recovered his spirit when it fell from the edge of the world and in a net of adoration and laughter freed him also in humility to adore. And if you say: 'Whose tale?' the answer is 'mine', but only in a not very good poem which I will re-write concerning the Lord Virgil of Mantua and set among the Taliessin poems...
In a letter of 1943,
   You know I always thought that art was not sanctity, and that sanctity was what mattered. 'At eventide' wrote St. John of the Cross, 'they will examine thee in love.' I shall not pass very well; in fact I shan't – but what else did the poem in Taliessin on the death of Virgil say?

Why Virgil?   i. '...no single poet has exercised over the poetic production of this country so long and so continuous a control as Virgil'. (*Virgil in English Poetry* by G. Gordon, 1931)

   ii. He exemplified the hazards of a poet's life as C. W. knew it, the experience of good things seen as horrible, obscene (C. W.):
      a. Augustus Caesar, patron – friend – enemy
      b. dark night of the soul, the Nightmare Death-in-Life (Coleridge) of words emptied of meaning; identity lost, (ll. 1-13 of 'Taliessin on the Death of Virgil').

Taliessin on the Death of Virgil

iii. Author of *Aeneid* – founding of Rome – life 'rooted in decencies of religion and of civilization' (C. W. *Story of the Aeneid*, introd. p. xiii, O.U.P. 1936) as C. W. in the matter of Britain in the Arthuriad, see annotation notes on 'Prelude'.

iv. Dante's leader through the Beatrician experience of love (*Divine Comedy*).

9-18. Charles found Alice's fall into Wonderland horrific. Man's most primitive fear is of falling?

17. Aeneas's journey across the Styx (river of death) full of pity and terror. See also notes on 'Vision of the Empire' and page 8 quotation from *Windows of Night*.

19. Pieties to Virgil would be 'honourable fulfilment of all moral duties – to the gods, one's country, family, friends' (C. W. *Story of the Aeneid*, introd. p. xii).

20-30. Time/Space twinned in simultaneity (Merlin/Brisen). 'To hold infinity in the palm of your hand And eternity in an hour' (Blake) makes possible, credible, C. W.'s ideas of exchange and substitution, e.g. Pauline's in *Descent into Hell*.

In more than 2000 years, Virgil has lived in us through his poetry, ministering to us in our joys, our sorrows, our fears. 'Others he saved'. His lovers, unknown to him and to one another, rush through time and space uniting in exchange of salvation. 'Himself he could not save.' The goodwill of the myriad little ordinary creatures has power to lift the glory, greater in its uniqueness than all of them together out of its despair of 'the spectral grave' and 'endless falling', and set it securely on the enduring monumental 'marble', pleading as they do so, that the poet will condescend to accept their help, in acknowledgement of their everlasting indebtedness to him, their friend, lover, and lord.

THE COMING OF PALOMIDES (T.S.)

Palomides, or Palamide, or Palamede, was

(i) Saracen knight, unbaptised, at Cornish court of King Mark; loves Queen Iseult, who loves Tristram and he her; befriended by Dinadan; has his victorious day; cheats Lancelot; pursues Blatant Beast (sex instinct run wild); finally baptised. (Malory's story)

(ii) Tutor to sons of King Lot and Queen Morgause of Orkney; pursues Questing Beast; figure of fun. (T. H. White's story)

(iii) Iseult ceded to him by King Mark, against her will,
                              he wist
More grace might come of that sweet mouth unkissed
Than joy for violence done it.

(Swinburne 'The Delivery of Iseult', 'one of the great Arthurian figures who awaits his due in verse' (C. W. in his Note on Swinburne's poem in *Victorian Narrative Verse*, O.U.P. 1927).

(iv) Traditional romantic rejected lover; comes 'softly', 'sweetly', 'shyly', a Galahad figure become capable of real love, to sit in the Perilous Chair in C. W.'s 'A Song of Palomides' in *Heroes and Kings*, Sylvan Press 1930.

From this state, realism began to replace romanticism in the life of the poet. There are three poems on Palomides in *Taliessin through Logres* which show this. No Virgil leads him like Dante to beatitude. He takes himself to hell and grovels there. And was it unknown pieties that came to rescue him? This poem is the first part of his saga.

Paragraph I:
8. Islam, and all non-Incarnational ideas have no union of God and matter.

12. Hazels: doctrines.

13. Coelius Vibenna: 'I looked up Mons Caelia on which Lateran stands; it was named after him, who was a leader of the Etruscans... They were said to be great in black magic (Goetry): hence 'Etruscan spells'' (C. W. Notes to Lewis).

The Coming of Palomides

23-27. In enquiries made before landing in Britain, Julius Caesar heard that Britain was an island of magic, to which came spirits of the dead and other spirits. Fishermen might become aware of shadowy shapes in the boat, and be compelled to row to shore; or hear unseen boats land and then silence.

II & III:
As Taliessin, on his return to Logres, saw a 'signalling hand', 'sickle of a golden arm', so Palomides coming to Logres 'saw an outstretched hand' and sang 'how curves of golden life define / the straightness of a perfect line' and so on to 'the single equilateral trine'. The trine is fact, emotion, knowledge (C. W. Notes to Lewis). For difference in metaphor compare Taliessin's and Palomides's upbringing and education. Letters at this period contain ideas of a beloved's arm, equilateral triangles, and geometrical figures. (See also Philip with Rosamund's arm in *Shadows of Ecstasy*.)

The poet is teased by Pythagorean principles and suggests that 'the world is built on number: mathematics (not scientifically used maths) is our key?' Thinks everybody has scalene triangle of his own (i.e. not equilateral). So, in third, fourth stanzas, he's got it. Eureka!

IV:
12. i. poetry, 'fire of mind'
   ii. mathematics, 'fire of fact'
   iii. love, 'fire of blood' . . . all in 'incredible obedience' to all
in 'true equilateral ease'. Through this perfect and equal relationship we ought to be able to proceed; the union of the three should push on through its own principle. I suppose it's a kind of analysis of the Fish in 'Bors to Elayne'.

VI:
9-10. Division stretched between / the queen's identity and the queen: the queen's identity is Queen in God as momentarily seen; when that light fails (see 'Prelude' last two lines) there is just the unillumined queen. 'And then the Questing Beast begins to do its fell work in us' (C. W. Notes to Lewis).

The Coming of Palomides

Reality cuts across Dantean ecstasy with the isosceles triangle; the two equal sides, echoes of twin roads ('Prelude'), desire for possession; obsession. Palomides is aware of his difference in colour, creed, culture – modern problems – and he is suddenly aware of the human (Iseult, Mark, Tristram) trio's inalienable indifference to himself, his aspirations, his potentialities, his poetry. As C. W. was so fond of quoting (from *Othello*):

> Not poppy, nor mandragora,
> Nor all the drowsy syrups of the world
> Shall ever medicine thee to that sweet sleep
> Which thou ow'dst yesterday.

LAMORACK AND THE QUEEN MORGAUSE (A. R.)

C. W.'s brief note explaining the place of Lamorack in the myth needs some expansion. He was brother to Percivale and Blanchefleur (Dindrane), and loved Queen Morgause, wife to King Lot of Orkney. Through her came the destruction of the Table, for as a result of the unknowing incest between herself and Arthur, Mordred was born. Her legitimate sons, Gawaine and Agravaine, killed their mother and Lamorack. C. W.'s note to Lewis says:

> L(amorack)'s love-affair is more a matter of terrible fate than Lancelot's; but I want L(amorack) in because of Gawaine killing his mother and L. and the feud with Lancelot. Gawaine is to be worldly honour run mad.

This part of the cycle, of course, was never written. There is a poem on Lamorack and Morgause in the original Arthurian cycle (see *Heroes and Kings*) in which Lamorack foresees the doom of the Table, but it describes a moment of erotic happiness, whereas the later poem is concerned almost wholly with 'terrible fate': from start to finish there is no hint of salvation. The pervasive symbolism is of primitive stone and primal catastrophe, 'the schism and first strife / of primeval rock with itself'. In Lamorack's vision, the queen is identified with this stone and its splitting, because of her destiny.

1. 'Livid' because bruised?

4. C. W.'s note: 'I fear the 'first flying creature' [*sic*, but presumably 'nature' as printed is correct] was meant only to be a pleasant comparison'.

7. Pre-Adamic: before the Fall; and then comes the catastrophe through the Queen.

18. Extreme theme: a double meaning; theme: province, and also action/meaning. C. W.'s note: 'All this is supposed [to be] at the time [of] and because of the dolorous blow, about which there will one day be a poem. It is contingency becoming actual to man'.

Lamorack and the Queen Morgause

20-24. Contingent: a thing that may happen. The Emperor foresees all that *may* come to be. The poem is obsessed by these shapes of horror, lying in the cleft (ll. 20, 29) or flying (ll. 36, 53, 80).

26. The Etruscan sorcerers pervert the true diviner's art. Lamorack sees the doom becoming actual; and then (l. 37 seq.) as it were goes back in time to a point before it has happened, and sees it foreshadowed in Morgause.

44. Canonical: legitimate.

47. After Balin had wounded King Pelles (the dolorous blow), perception was darkened and identities confused.

53-56. The Adam: before the Fall a single noun describes the two natures. I am not sure whether in the 'whirling creature' (see the 'flying nature' of the first stanza) C. W. is thinking of Milton's winged Satan. The result of the Adam's demand for knowledge was that God himself, whom Adam already knew as good, had to be known as evil.

57 et seq. Looking into Morgause's eyes, 'a dark cavern', Lamorack sees her history unfold. Arthur is the 'crowned man without eyes' (he committed incest without knowing that the woman was his half-sister, i.e. blindly), and the place is between his palace at Caerleon and Carbonek, the castle of the hallows, which must be (as C. W. says in *Arthurian Torso*, p. 81) 'if not in, at least on the borders of Broceliande'.

64. His own face: Arthur's sin was to make another in his own image – as Wentworth in *Descent into Hell*? – and the 'light feet' of l. 62 emphasizes the unreality of the exchange. The woman too is eyeless, blind, but it is possible that she is only *thought* to be blind by Arthur. See Vinaver's Malory, Bk. I, ch. xix. In any case, the act is a ghastly parallel to the intercourse of Lancelot with Helayne which produced Galahad, the saviour.

Lamorack and the Queen Morgause

66. The Great Ban: C. W.'s note: 'Yes — prohibition and excommunication', for incest. (He also says: 'Blast! I had forgotten': possibly Lewis had reminded him that there is a King Ban in the Arthurian legend — an association quite irrelevant to the cycle.)

67-68. The blatant beast, the sex instinct run wild, is let loose through the act of incest. See also 'Palomides before his Christening'.

69 et seq. The figure is a parody of true love, and it is close to the City itself.

73 et seq. The child is Mordred, the destroyer. Lamorack remains 'the queen's servant', and his mission was begun in obedience to the king's word (l. 13): now, it is his fate never to be free from the terrible vision.

BORS TO ELAYNE: THE KING'S COINS (A. R.)

A poem about true exchange. Bors, the married man, earning his living in a regular job, typifies Exchange on the Way of Affirmation; therefore he is one of the three to achieve the Grail.

9. The colour of corn: A.M.H. tells me that C. W. said the comparison was hackneyed, and vague because 'no one knows exactly what the colour of corn is'. And the hands are doctrine itself. Lewis must have found some difficulty in the passage, for C.W. comments:
> I don't believe I can explain 'their doctrine –' etc. The hands always seem to me incredibly significant; and Bors feels that Elaine's hands have a power of doctrine in them more than the theological schools of Gaul. But cf. the hands in the *Vision of Empire*. 'The power of man seems to me wound on your thumbs (which are like old heroes and saints to me) as on a winch.'

24-25. All are both givers and receivers.
Day of the turn: the day when each takes his turn?

34. The king (Arthur Pendragon) has a dragon for crest.

43. The head stamped on the coins: Bors has a vision of disaster, as Lamorack in the previous poem. Here it is brought about by trade pursued for its own sake rather than for mutual good. C. W.'s comment:
> 'The social order can only be founded on this intense appreciation of exchange as opposed to unillumined contracts'. So, though Kay says complacently 'Gold dances deftly across frontiers', Taliessin sees the danger. 'When the means are autonomous, they are deadly' – when any medium, any means of expression, is valued most for its own sake (when politicians, for instance, mouth phrases that do not correspond with any reality – a danger that was very apparent in the nineteen-thirties when the poem was written – or when Money is made into a god), we are lost.

Bors to Elayne: On the King's Coins

75. The Archbishop then enlarges the theme – that we can only live, or die, through others.

84. While the unrighteous world has its day, 'this world', i.e. those called to be saints, can only make the best of it, transforming it to a true exchange. For these, money is *a* medium of exchange, not *the* medium, as Kay put it.

93. Ass-eared Midas comes in aptly, as it was his greed that brought on him the curse of the golden touch. (Ovid, *Metamorphoses* II.5)

95. The freely-made compact is turning into the rigidity of contract, where each demands his 'right': will earn and pay, but not receive and give. Trade Union tyranny comes to the mind of a present-day reader. The poem ends with a prayer that the dying social order may yet be redeemed.

It may be worth recalling here that I heard W. H. Auden, at the end of one of his lectures as Poetry Professor at Oxford, put down his script and say by heart the passage beginning 'We had a good thought...'

THE STAR OF PERCIVALE (R. W.)

The emblem of Percivale is a star. His star was Venus, = Phosphor and Hesper, the morning and evening star. In the two previous poems, the beginning of separations is seen in Logres, but in 'The Star of Percivale' we are shown that something else is springing up. Logres may be failing, but there is work for the king's poet's household to do.

1-7. Percivale stands at the western door (magical because the King's Hall was said to have been raised by Merlin by magical power), playing his harp. He makes music of his vision, intellectual and substituted love. Taliessin outside in the court among the people makes poetry which uses that music to see love in human terms, but in its own nature as well as in its beginning in each young heart. He uses a harp that another has played. C. S. Lewis in 'Williams and the Arthuriad' says: he is 'living as all artists do in another's house of art' (p. 136).

8-9. A serving maid is beguiled by his song and she runs to him in adoration, thinking she loves the man because his song shows her the nature of love. Taliessin turns her devotion from himself to the vision and nature of love, a spiritual obedience.

12. *Acts* XIV.15: Paul and Barnabas in Lystra.

20-22. The Archbishop (Dubric) sees in her face that she has seen 'the light of Christ's glory'.

23. Dubric: (St. Dubricius, d. 612). Geoffrey of Monmouth in 9th Book of *Historia* describes how Arthur is crowned King of Britain by Dubricius Archbishop of Caerleon.

25-28. Vision of a new kingdom in Logres has to be worked out in daily life, exactly like the life of love. But this also tends, at times, to become personal and the clearness of the vision to be clouded.

29-32. Logothete: in C. W.'s usage is angel, messenger, though its original meaning was auditor or Byzantine functionary.

Chlamys: a short flowing cape.

33-36. In contrast to 20-22, inside the chapel as they kneel at the mass, they think of their own preoccupations. Balin feels only his anger. Arthur worships his own achievement, and Lancelot only a representation of the Queen, the symbol, not love itself.

THE ASCENT OF THE SPEAR (R. W.)

1-7. Taliessin in the palace yard finds that the same girl who was so suddenly converted in the previous poem has relapsed and has been put in the stocks for brawling with a fellow servant in the King's hall.

15-24. Taliessin addresses her in high courteous fashion — 'did we not together adore'. She answers roughly.

25-33. He removes her resentment. She admits the justice of her punishment. She denies pride.

38. C. W.'s note: 'The Caucasian theme throb' means, *ad hoc*, that, but also the whole ache of the body and all that in the difficult acceptance of the Way of order, morals, discipline, instruction. Caucasia is more than the buttocks'.

49-52. Sir Kay, the steward, sends a message offering her release if she is a friend of Taliessin's. Her pride at first refuses pardon but is subdued by Taliessin's use of (ll. 66-67) Augustine's words 'Love and do what you choose'. She accepts release.

79-80. Pheidippides was sent by the Athenians to solicit Spartan help against the Persians who had landed at Marathon in 490 B. C. He covered 150 miles in 2 days. After the victory he was chosen to carry the news to Athens. The exertions of the first run, and of the battle, caused him to stumble, fall exhausted, and die after giving the good news.

THE SISTER OF PERCIVALE

C. W.'s Note:
> The slave with the scar carries on the idea of battle and discipline in honour. The 'bright fork' is summer lightning. T. is between the world of sensation and the world of spirit. He identifies the girl's body and the eastward Empire (as the body), and he knows the Caucasian dangers. But he also sees arm and spine and so on as the radii of – of the half-circle; what is the *full* circle? how do we find it? It must be everywhere, yet ... [*sic*] And this kind of thing is felt at such moments as seeing someone drawing water or handing a book or whatever; only water has a suggestion of images and reflections and nourishment and fertility. Her shoulders carry labour (as, in 'Coming of Galahad', happy discipline). At this moment T. (fortunate fellow!) hears the trumpet go off, with which he identifies also the movement of her arm. He sees her and Blanchefleur together, as sisters, twins, categories, but the back of sensation changes into the face of exchange-in-love, which is like, say, (the Back of) God himself. The hemispheres change, but he feels that the one half-circle has closed with the other to make a full circle – 'the transit of Venus'. Blanchefleur could hardly be perfect to understanding without the slave, though the whole principle is more clear and advanced in her than in the slave ... The scar and the star are the same identity in two categories. Hence T's outburst. B's greeting (like Beatrice's) is the always-approaching, never reaching relation of the divine part to the divine whole.

Further notes by A.M.H.

Title: Percivale: his sister Blanchefleur is called Dindrane in later poems. C. W. said he thought 'Blanchefleur' too literary. She died through giving blood to a woman who was dying and lived by the transfusion, a pure example of substitution. Blanchefleur's body was the only thing of this world which was taken by Galahad, Percivale, and Bors in the ship sailing to the city of Sarras in the land of the Trinity.

The Sister of Percivale

1-3. Horizon of sensation: your vision, boundary, NOT your position or place.

North: to Logres, from the spine to the head (see *T.T.L.* map), the intellect meaning the 'feeling intellect' also (see next poem line 53). Taliessin idling on the wall of the courtyard of the entrance to Camelot.

Fork: a touch not of earth. It flicked the solid buildings and his boundary of vision.

5-6. Sloth: here means a habit become a condition.

Idleness: a temporary relaxation.

Troth of ambiguous verse: a meeting of two or double meanings in verse.

8. Scarred: by discipline or suffering.

10. Scar: of discipline, result of correction by the hazel of measurement (see next poem ll. 49-51), bringing results and growth.

15. Percivale was called 'li Galois' meaning 'from Wales', his duchy.

18. Horizon: her ideas, thoughts, vision.

19-21. The world: means also the body; also the basis of life, balance, and justice.

Themes: mean areas of the Empire and also significances of parts of the body ('ambiguous verse').

22. Geometrical images become part of the ambiguity, implying accuracy and relation to the creating plan.

26-27. Can we know what relationship our experiences bear to creative power and love?

28-30. Trumpet sound is full and clear with the breath of the trumpeter as the slave's arm is with flesh, each fashioned exactly as

The Sister of Percivale

in geometry.

31-33. New fate: for Taliessin, who yet has not known this kind of love. Its call struck him as the slave's action completed the geometric pattern.

34. Her other arm doubled the direct sound of the trumpet. The voice of Percivale blended in Taliessin's hearing with the trumpet.

37-38. Taliessin heard the trumpet call and saw the face of Blanchefleur.
   Hemispheres: the half of the earth's circle which at any moment remains unseen, from whatever point on the surface you stand, became visible by an experience he had never before known.

41. The other side of experience, the undiscovered meaning, for a moment became known to Taliessin – perhaps experience and meaning.

42. Back in the Mount: refers to the experience of Moses when God spoke to him on Mount Sinai; though he could not look on God's face and survive, God allowed him to see His back (*Exodus* XXXIII.30-33).

45. Red track: suggests scar from suffering or a beating for discipline; it now shows, in love, as a mark of glory.

46. Percivale and Taliessin are spoken of as poets, 'brothers in the grand art' in next poem l. 219.

48. The exactness of the universe, geometrically patterned in the sound of the trumpet and the bone of the arm.

49-51. Friendly jokes. 'Caucasian journeys' could mean love-affairs or acquaintances with girls.
   Stress of the Empire: worries of administration.
   Greek minuscula: Shorter Oxford Eng. Dict. gives *minuscule*, many meanings, small, opposite to capital or uncial, small cursive

script developed from the uncial, a 7th Century manuscript in this writing. Perhaps a joking reference to study and learning.

53-54. Transit of Venus: Everyman's Encyclopaedia gives: 'Venus's passage across the sun's disc at inferior conjunction, is a rare phenomenon, and occurs about 6 June or 7 December.' Has occurred 12 times since 1631 when first observed in England. C.W. was delighted with this phrase as an offering to one's beloved. The connection with Venus and the scar suggests that the scar was discipline and the discipline was Love's. It links up with the poem 'The Ascent of the Spear', l. 43, where the girl is persuaded to obedience by mention of Venus, Percivale's planet. See also l. 45 in this poem and throughout this poem.

55. Scars: discipline.
    Lightnings: vision as in l. 3.
    Wheel: perhaps Fortune (or chance or luck)'s wheel in the Inferno l. 96 of Dante's *Divine Comedy*. Perhaps linked with the creamed-with-crimson sphere, 'Taliessin in the School of the Poets', verse 6.

56. I have never clearly understood this line. I can only think now that it means 'all preparation is over and now the work begins.'

57. The sound breaks from the trumpet which is straight like the bone, and one gets a sound from the working in union of all the different modes of experience.

58. Eyed axis of both horizons: full circle of creative power on any scale, fully observant and (I think, here) observed.

59. The well's rope's wheel which brings up the weight of water for the stooping water-carrier; the wheel must be the wheel of line 55, which, when in any experience fully revolves and its energy generates the full circle of creative power, produces the mental and emotional and spiritual illumination in its action.

61. The circle is the whole, the diameter only the half.

Asymptote: Shorter Oxford English Dictionary gives: 'a line which continually approaches a given curve, but does not meet it within a finite distance'. Clearly a welcome image to C. W. of the best of human love. Again a mathematical image, such as was close to his vision of love and creative power shown in this poem, and glimpsed in many others.

63. Infinite decimal: roughly, a recurring decimal, no finish to its process. C. W. once referred to the decimal as an image of the unit of measurement through Creation, containing all distance and capacity, large or small.

THE SON OF LANCELOT

C. W.'s Note:
> 'Nimue' etc. Along 'measurement' Merlin ses the third heaven, which is that of accomplished states of being, and is as far as human understanding can go. Nimue (anthropotokos, but not imagined formally as theotokos) = Broceliande, is the source of time and space and great ideas and images; she is, in the universe, the principle of the 'feeling intellect', which (though I discovered it afterwards) is not unlike Palomides' triangle. When intellect and emotion are proportioned and immediate and lasting and gracious. One might say it is nature, adoration, and madness seen finally. 'There is no variableness' – as, they say, there is not in the Spiritual Marriage. Merlin himself only dimly apprehends this – as sound; he has to come back a little way to do his job.

Further notes by A.M.H. and A. S.

Poem is concerned with coinherence and substitution, and with the opposite state of self-preservation by fear, enmity, greed, degradation. Christ has established substitution, but choice or rejection of the way remain with each man. Sin and fear still separate man from Christ and from man. His capacity for Christ is potential but often not actual. In the poem an act of substitution brings the capacity for Christ into man's life. The wolf theme is man out for himself. Only the wolf legend connected with the founding of Rome is good, as the Roman City is taken as the foundation of European order and civilisation.

I:
1-4. Lupercalia (Latin for wolf – lupus) was festival (Feb. 15) in honour of the wolf that suckled Romulus and Remus who grew up to found and build the city of Rome; one object of it was fertility, women without children crowded to be touched by the thongs of the priests. Rhea Silvia was mother of the twins, a vestal virgin who was forced by Mars the god of battle.
    Aeneid: poem by Virgil of another legend of founding of Rome,

The Son of Lancelot

by Prince Aeneas of Troy after Troy had been captured.

5-6. Sense of sin and incapacity hid the way of substitution opened by Christ and left even Christian man with terror of 'the God' and of guilt.

Confiteor: the confession of sin by the people in the church's liturgy.

7. Wolves, now images of guerillas and pirates and personal enmities, ranged Roman Europe and Christian-Arthurian Britain and Camelot.

II:
1. Search for understanding by learning, insight, specialised knowledge, prayer.

2. Quinquagesima: a name for the last Sunday before Lent in the Church's year. Early in the year, chilly ('thin night air'); the Church of England's collect for this day is well known and was a particular strength to C. W.: 'O Lord, who has taught us that all our doings without charity are nothing worth; send thy Holy Ghost, and pour into our hearts that most excellent gift of Charity, the very bond of peace and of all virtues, without which whosoever liveth is counted dead before Thee; grant this for thine only Son Jesus Christ's sake.' C. W. felt the last sentence 'without which' etc. with intense realism.

3. Chamber of union: chamber where Lancelot was to lie, under drugs and in darkness, with 'Helayne, supposed Guinevere' and so by this substitution to produce Galahad; also the union of prayer, vision, and knowledge.

4. Horny sight: unclear, thick, only seeing worldly things. Pre-glass windows were made of thin plates of horn.

8. High grades: higher levels of vision and life, familiar in the learning of the Jewish and other ancient cultures.

The Son of Lancelot

14. Desecrated parallels: C. W. said you could see this as the web of coinherence used for tyranny and gain.

21. Tidal figures: not stable, moved by personal ambitions, sufferings.

25. Thurible: an incense container, sign here of outward ceremony.

25-26. Magic throws no truck with dreams: is not concerned with day-dreaming. See later in this poem, where the sleeping nuns preserve a dreamless adoration. Study of God, for good or for bad is concerned with reality, fact, not how you fancy it.

29. Harried God and the soul: a continuing theme in C. W.'s poetry, Islam denies the Incarnation and maintains that God is One, that matter and flesh have no permanence, glory, or resurrection.

38. Heat's pallor's secret: the passion and intensity found by some who choose the Way of Rejection, of chastity and poverty. Fires lit mean convents founded.

40. Verulam: Roman name for St. Albans (where C. W. was brought up and educated) the place of the English martyr Alban.

III:
3. An arm to a sickle: in the previous poem it was an arm to a bucket. The application of daily life, love's means, methods, works, to love and service.

4. Third sphere: in Dante's *Paradiso* this is Venus, Percivale's star. C. W. links it with Wordsworth (northern poet) writing of 'the feeling intellect', that union within Creation that C. W. searched to express. (*Prelude* XIV, l. 226)

11. Last reach: third sphere is as far as magic (hazel rod of divination) can achieve.
    Fixed is the full: no deterioration will take place.

The Son of Lancelot

18. Tritosphere: normal sight's three dimensions.

IV:

1. Pelles was the hereditary (of the line of Joseph of Arimathea, *via* the legend of Glastonbury in England) Keeper of the Grail. Carbonek is in the west of England, and the place of dedication, inspiration, and holiness, but still earthly.

2. Dolorous blow: the origin of sin in the Arthurian myth. In Malory's *Morte D'Arthur*, Bk. II, ch. 31, section 15, Sir Balyn stops at a castle, meets the invisible (? dark, as in 'dark horse') knight Garlon, with whom he has a quarrel, and kills him in the castle hall. King Pellam, owner of the castle, fights Sir Balyn for the crime of fighting in the hall, and killing a knight. King Pellam (Malory's spelling) broke Sir Balyn's sword, and Sir Balyn ran through the castle looking for a weapon, followed by the King. He entered 'a chamber marvellously rich, and a bed with cloth of gold, and one lying therein, and a table of clean gold. And upon the table stood a marvellous spear strangely wrought'. (Malory's words, condensed A.M.H.) Sir Balyn, in spite of this obvious sanctity, seized the spear and wounded King Pellam, who fell down, and the castle walls fell down and Sir Balyn fell down. In fact, the Fall, in an image: a holy thing used for personal gain. The Blow has continuous results in each person, each age, pain and inability.

4. Woman's under the moon: monthly menstruation. The Dolorous Blow could not be healed until the coming of Galahad.

7. Wolf-month: month of Mars, father of Romulus and Remus, March.

10. The climax of the poem. Brisen is Merlin's sister, in a sense Space, Opportunity, as he is Time, History. Helayne was the daughter of King Pelles (Pellam) and so in the hereditary line of Keepers of the Grail. Sir Lancelot's love was dedicated to Queen Guinevere, and to his friend King Arthur. All his belief in honour and the vows of knighthood as ways of self-discipline, following Christ, and service of man, was involved in this faithful love.

The Son of Lancelot

13. Lycanthropy: Shorter Oxford English Dict. gives 'a kind of insanity in which the patient imagines himself to be a wolf'. Also a kind of witchcraft in which human beings were supposed to assume form and nature of wolf.

V:

6-7. Seed of love's ambiguity, . . . taunt and truth: Lancelot's son Galahad; by unmeant infidelity (to Guinevere) L. begot the capacity for fidelity and true love, Galahad.

VI:

1-4. The whole Empire contracted . . . there only warmth dilated: The first statement of the theme of pain and effort leading to triumph through new birth which is developed through the second part of the poem. Helayne's labour and the birth and rescue of Galahad are paralleled by the Empire's distress and the rescue of Caucasia by the Emperor.

5 et seq. Savage unbridled instincts and the denial of the redeemed unity of body and soul alike threaten to destroy the proper relationship between man and God. With physical and intellectual responses both twisted out of their proper shape it seems that even the generation of new life will lose its holiness.

Historically, the Moslems were masters of the Straits of Gibraltar.

8. Manes, or Mani, was the third century founder of the religion of Manichaeism which was to exert a heretical influence on Christian doctrine for a thousand years. It was violently dualistic, proclaiming the perpetually antagonistic existence of two equal supreme principles, one good and the other evil. Matter was created by the evil principle and spirit by the good so that their union in redeemed humanity, and still more the union of divinity and humanity in 'the twy-natured single Person' of Christ, was unthinkable.

9. Lupercal: the City; Lateran: the Church.

The Son of Lancelot

22. The birth of the child who is to achieve the Grail reveals the glory of the flesh once again.

26 et seq. Arthur and Guinevere had both forsaken their vocations: his to serve the Grail, hers to be a faithful wife.

VII:
17. Tall form: 'The blessed young sorcerer', Merlin deliberately takes the form of a wolf through the power of his mind as Lancelot had unknowingly done through the overthrow of his mind.

28 et seq. The knowledge of Merlin embraces City, Church, 'irony, and defeated irony' and brings them all to the rescue of Galahad.

31. Love's means to love: the instrument of which divine love makes use in order to fulfil its loving purposes. The vocation of every servant of God is to be precisely this. See l. 229.

VIII:
1 et seq. Straight narrative, finishing with perhaps the most pictorial and touching line and a half in the whole work.

IX:
7-12. Natural instincts controlled and therefore happy and blessed: contrasted with 'the red carnivorous violation of intellectual love' in VII, 8-9.

X:
23-26. 'We bring news of great joy;
 now in this world we servants love;
 the sweet city is being built;
 because Love who loves is being loved'.
I do not know whether C. W. invented or found this quatrain.

PALOMIDES BEFORE HIS CHRISTENING

C. W.'s Note:
   Romantic love and social order have both become entirely blank. All that there is at all is hardness and the itch and scratchings on the rock. But Dinadan realizes that loss may be a greater possession than having; and P., who would be quite incapable of believing believingly believes unbelievingly, by means of that more-than-irony.

Further notes by T. S.

[Letter of C. W. 1930: 'The wise man is he who is glad to be loved as a kindness . . . three degrees of love − i. that in which you were first, ii. ...one of a few, iii. ...weren't there at all − or hardly. And only when you could rejoice in being iii. could you be said to *love*. But No. i has a bit of a pull!'] Had Charles in mind to show a Dantean Beatification through unrequited love? But Iseult was alive, constantly under Palomides's eye, with husband, lover, friends. (See 'Coming of Palomides'.)

1-8. Flash forward to moment of escape from mental bolt-hole, when wheel has (ll. 75-78) come full-circle.

4. Slant-eyes: a. astrology comes from east
   b. state of mind when one looks, and is looked at, askance.

4, 76. Caerleon: city of astrologers? (Geoffrey of Monmouth).

5. Astrologers studied stars as occult, astronomers as exact, science.

6-8. Desolate landscape infers annihilation of spirit − food for neither fact nor fancy.

9-12. Creative mind, ranging Broceliande intent on its own will, looses and is itself trapped by a more dangerous beast (ll. 84-89) than Malory's. (*Morte D'Arthur*, IX.12)

Palomides before His Christening

9-24. Palomides relates facts and failure of his intention to show the world that the unbaptised Saracen is the superior in intellect and chivalry of the best Christian knights.

17. As Arthur wrecks things by mistakenly supposing kingdoms are for kings, so P. in thinking Love is for lovers. 'Adored for love's sake be immortal Love...' (sonnet by C. W.).

24. Indulges in malice.

25-32. Boomerang. Bees (in bonnets) etc. buzzing in dissolution of Iseult's flesh, but the crowd's wonder at his cunning would cover that.

33-40. It does not. His disordered mind seeks escape from the city's discipline. (See *Taliessin through Logres* 'Prelude', sixth stanza: and Wentworth going down into himself in *Descent into Hell*.) Palomides climbs upward through Iseult's skeleton. (C. W. says somewhere that physical delight should grow inwards; that to measure the beloved's frame is to measure the Empire, and P. had made that actual journey from Ispahan to Logres.)

45-64. With and beyond bones, brain works for comfort with others' phantasies; cherishing the beast; luxuriating in concupiscence, whipping up dying desire (as Wordsworth's widow with her dead grief); imagination straining to beget upon itself fresh images from old delights – cates – dainties (Shakespeare).

65-68. Still resists light of common day.

69-72. Cf. Lily Sammile suckling dead in *Descent into Hell*.

73-90. Bats: now fear of madness makes him move at last, to look beyond himself. All is as it was, but seen now as it is, he cannot understand the fuss he made.

81. Chi-Rho: symbol formed from first two letters of Christ in Greek, signifying Christianity, as on converted Emperor Constan-

Palomides before His Christening

tine's helmet, etc.

83-84. Possible salvation or certain damnation.

89 et seq. Only Dinadan cares, the lone joker laughing either way; but like Palomides an outsider.

THE COMING OF GALAHAD (A. R.)

For this difficult poem the notes made by C. W. for C. S. Lewis are quite full, and I shall quote them in my annotation. See also Lewis in *The Figure of Arthur*, pp. 166-72, though I think he is not right in one or two points.

I:
1. In the hall...: Malory, Book XIII, tells of the coming of Galahad to Camelot (not Caerleon as C. W. says in his printed note, but the difference is not important): how he sat in the Perilous Chair; how the Grail appeared and each knight had the food he liked best; and how Galahad was set in the king's bed. Even as a young man, in the notes which he made in his Commonplace Book, C. W. had had the idea that each knight preferred just what was set before him – as Taliessin in line 90 of this poem.

3. Galahad, man's capacity for Christ, is set in place of the old Adam.

7. 'I wolde fayne se hym,' seyde the quene, 'for he muste nedys be a noble man for so hys fadir ys that hym begate' (Malory, XIII.4).

II:
While the lords go up to the Rite, Taliessin goes down through the palace (the body) to the lowest offices: from there, the necessary place of excrement, he looks upward at the lights of the procession. As Galahad is set in Arthur's bed, the vows of love made by Arthur, Guinevere, and Lancelot are fulfilled by the 'third heaven', the sphere of Venus, though not in the way they intended. 'This is the result of talking about love, as it always is. We get Galahad instead of what we wanted' (C. W.).

III:
3. Porphyry stair: cf. 'Vision of the Empire' line 10. Galahad is to supplant his father – perhaps a reminiscence of Henry V trying on his father's crown.

The Coming of Galahad

5. A youth...: Malory, Book VII, describes how Gareth worked for a year as a scullion (in Malory, he is unknown to Gawaine as to the rest).

V:
6. The Great Ban: the excommunication of Arthur because of his incest.

VI:
4. In *The Prelude* Book V, Wordsworth describes how in a dream he met a Bedouin carrying a stone (mathematics) and a shell (poetry), which he is trying to save from a flood which pursues him. C. W. explains stone and shell as
> the hard exploration of romantic states and the beauty of romantic states. The beauty comes before and after; which is why the shell has to be fitted to the stone, to breed there, and afterwards bursts from the stone (see line 158); this is the finding of Identity. Galahad is the supreme of both states.

Taliessin has heard of this from the Druids; Gareth has heard Wordsworth's poem read, and has himself had a vision of a girl as the bearer of stone and shell, measurement and all sound, who barely escapes from the corruption of fallen Logres.

VIII:
1. Galahad unites stone and shell – see above.

5. The five houses, or cells: C. W.'s comment: 'There is no experience of man in which these shell and stone experiences do not exist; T. mentions five: poetry and wisdom, sex, intellect and theology, religion, interior religion'.

9. The double newels: see 'Taliessin in the School of the Poets', line 50.

IX:
2. Gareth endures his humiliation for the sake of the City. How can man experience choice, if he has not the knowledge of what is to be rejected? Gareth is the agent of this process.

The Coming of Galahad

X:
4. (I chose) the good that was there in front of me. 'When I could have anything I wanted, I wanted nothing but what was there' (C.W.).

XI:
1. When Taliessin tried to relate his first experiences of his five 'cells' to later ones, 'when he tried to find their *reality*, the shells became empty' (C. W.); the pentagram was simply five isolated points; the hazel rod, instrument of order, had nothing to measure.

12. But the slave girl reminds him that the hazel rod means discipline, and that there is blessing in suffering ('sharp style', rod for writing as well as beating) freely accepted. She, accepting the cut hazel's chastisement may discover the uncut, the fruit, which is the colour of Galahad's eyes.
   We cannot *know* the full meaning of our experience, but can take it to heart, rejecting the cynical 'Who cares?'

21. Galahad is the transmuted measure of all.

XII:
5. C. W.'s comment: 'He talks of her hand as if he were in love with it, but then T. can see the glory everywhere; he sees the light on Caucasia without desiring to possess it. But I think he has loved Blanchefleur chiefly'.

7. Scavenger to the king's substitute: Gareth to Galahad.

XIII:
9 et seq. Guinevere's jealousy because of Lancelot's supposed unfaithfulness shows in her eyes, her hand becomes a grasping claw, measurement measures only itself in a vain repetition.

XIV:
1 et seq. I am not sure of the meaning here, but I think that in answer to the girl's question about how to die, Taliessin gives her the affirmations that should be made. Proofs – perhaps the proofs

The Coming of Galahad

he has just given of the nature of love; roofs, the 'houses' he has spoken of (XI, l. 1 and l. 3). He goes on to describe the four zones which divide the empire from the empyrean (a reminiscence of the *Paradiso* here, though they are not quite as Dante). C. W.'s own note on this is as follows – with my additions in brackets: 'There is a preference (Venus) = Gareth, the hazel; and of irony (Jupiter) = perhaps Palomides; and irony that is something more = Dinadan; and of Galahad (Saturn) 'turned space' and time, cf. next poem, 'The Departure of Merlin'.' Elsewhere, C. W. speaks of the irony of Dinadan as irony defeated, because understood and accepted.

12. The glory bursts from all attempts to measure it?

14. The taunt: the deception that drove Lancelot mad, and produced Galahad. The original 'taunt' was thrown by passers-by at Jesus on the cross: 'He saved others, himself he cannot save'. It was true, but in a way that the passers-by did not think of.

15. The sphere of Jupiter is also justice. Logres with the coming of Galahad is now there, and all planets and provinces of the Empire circle round Galahad's sphere, the sphere of Saturn. This in medieval thought was the sphere of the ascetic contemplatives. See *Paradiso* Canto XXI.

XV:
1-2. 'But Taliessin's eyes are non-human; he sees 'the Throne' and his eyes resemble the Throne' (C. W.).

THE DEPARTURE OF MERLIN (J. W.)

1-2. Lateran's stone: the stone altar, with its embedded relics.

Vicarious hands: 'done for' another. Here, as the Vicar of Christ, he consecrates the elements for all men.

The Pope: 'The Pope was in possession of Rome; about both his figure and that of the remote Emperor in Byzantium there lay something of a supernatural light – at best mystical, at worst magical' (*Arthurian Torso*, p. 80).

6. Moslem and Manichaean: heresies (i) of the denial of the Incarnation and (ii) that Satan was co-eternal with God.

7. The Table: the Round Table, perhaps made by Merlin for the 150 Knights. Merlin set an empty chair among the others round the Table, to be the 'Perilous throne' or 'chair' of Galahad: see the last line of this poem.

17-20. Joseph of Nazareth: a foster-father who recedes from Biblical narrative when his work is done, as must Merlin.

Joseph of Arimathea: the legend was that he received the blood of Christ in a cup at the Crucifixion. Another foster-father, but here also connected with the blood of Christ.

25. Rites and runes: one of the references to Merlin as a magician. 'Astrology . . . that each man, being unique, was a unique image of the universe, . . . a high and learned science; it was forbidden for good reasons, but it was not fatalistic'. ('Index of the Body', *Dublin Review* 1942)

32. Flat djongs: the sea-wood of Broceliande stretched to alien P'o-Lu, so here the wooden galley is contrasted with the enemy craft.

41-42. Dryad: a wood nymph who inhabits a tree, a spirit of the tree.

Hazel and elm, oak and bamboo: the meaning of the woods. The hazel-rod of measurement; elm and oak were usual building

The Departure of Merlin

woods, apart form their poetical implications; bamboo a reference to P'o-Lu.

49. Nimue, lady of lakes and seas: one of the figures in the myth developed by Swinburne in 'Tristram of Lyonesse', a poem much admired by Charles Williams. A complex image of Nature coming from the wood of Broceliande.

THE DEATH OF PALOMIDES (T. S.)

Taliessin through Logres reaches climax in 'Coming of Galahad':
Palomides christened; Galahad 'sat in the perilous sell'; appearance
of Grail; companions aware of co-inherence.

In following poem, Merlin, work accomplished, spins himself
off into the 'simultaneity of time'. (Recollect discussing Einstein,
Dunne – speed of light, relativity of time, many dimensions, etc.).
Next, death comes to Palomides. Surely this poem is a superb
example of 'recollection in tranquillity' despite challenge of final
'If', reminding us of the arrogance of the young Saracen (C. W.'s
notes), the unbelieving belief (*ibid.*) of the Christian convert.
Resigned, he came to baptism, sure only that whatever sort of fool
he looked, it would be nothing to the fool he would be, if he
followed the jealous beast into Hell, Dante's 'good of intellect'
denied.

1-4. As in previous Palomides poem, poet starts with present point,
his final integration with kingdom, power, and glory, flashing back
(ll. 6-24) to point of departure leading to Logres, Iseult,
Christianity.

5. Mohammed; Alla il Alla.

6-8. In Spain, Islam allied with Judaism against Christianity.
(*Descent of the Dove*, p. 93; Gibbon *Decline*, Book V).

8. Monsalvat, Monsalvasch, Monserrat: 8th century monastery;
miracle-working image of Virgin Mary; later connected with Grail
legends. (Eschenbach: Wagner)

13-16. See 'Coming of Palomides'.

17-18. 'Seed-mail = chain-mail, seed-pearls, springing seed, youth,
young arrogant militancy' (C. W.'s notes to Lewis).

19-24. Young creature, avid for knowledge, feels strength of
garnered wisdom of ancient faiths.

20. Netzach: station on Sephirotic tree (Jewish cosmic diagram) denotes Victory. (Sephardim: Spanish, Portuguese Jews.)

25. Now to the present...

29. 'Paths and stations – We are free from the sense of finality except in the End' (C. W.'s notes to Lewis).

30-32. Mistaking worldly speed for other-worldly, in his love for Iseult? Thinking he was making more than angelical speed; could afford to linger because he had already arrived? (Dante with Virgil in Purgatory?) Dinadan knowing journey had hardly begun.

40. Eagle: pre-eminent in myth, folklore. Symbol, at once, of immortality and temporal power (Ancient Greece); in Christian myth, St. John, one of the four 'creatures' in 'Revelation'. Chief of Charles's angelic manifestations, wisdom and balance, in *Place of Lion*.

41. 'In my end is my beginning'. Lady Julian.

44. Unbelieved symbol: the Cross.

45-56. Palomides recollects, renounces, is reconciled, with a gesture of ineffable grace, 'in a passion of patience', Taliessin's rule.
    At first we did not expect profit or praise;
    we were far too honourable or haughty for the pitpat
    of the world; we knew about, we enjoyed, irony.
    But we did not think irony would desert to the other side.

    And as for love – that indeterminate prospect –
    it was not so secure as irony, but more kind...
    until we found it was not so kind to us
    as our own impulse had supposed, by its nature it would be;
    and what besides love or irony had we designed?

C. W.: 1 April 1938

PERCIVALE AT CARBONEK (A. R.)

The poem is about Galahad's coming to Carbonek, where he is to heal the wounded king (Malory VIII.19 et seq). Charles's letter of 15 February 1935 describes his first conception of the poem – the textual variants from the final version are also of interest:

I've altered – or at least – added to Malory a little point. Meditating on the Riding of Galahad, it suddenly occurred to me last night to put the High Prince at the ... but you may as well have the first stanza –

Galahad stood in the gate of Carbonek;
the folk of Pelleas ran to greet him;
Christ was before him, behind the rent silk of the sun.
    His eyes were vacant; he sighed Bless me, Lord Lancelot.
And so on; and then –
Christ was before him; reconciliation waited;
Arthur and Pelleas waited the end of their schism;
Grief rose in his heart; Galahad wept
    for the need of his birth and the doubled misery of Logres.

On the threshold of Carbonek the High Prince doubted,
his fibre torn by the infelicities of time

Only once does the Joyous Prince weep, and that is when he comes to Carbonek, the place where he was born, and Lancelot went mad. And even Galahad doubts if even eternity is quite worth it. But at least he implores his father to forgive him – not Lancelot alone, but Arthur and all Logres; as Percivale, whose poem it is, says – the High Prince being incapable of speech:

I commended the Prince to my lord Sir Lancelot his father...

The feet of Lancelot running, running, running...

Angelic were they (the folk of Pelleas) or faery; all myrmidons
of unremitted beauty; astonished they stood.
The High Prince fell on his knees in the gate of Carbonek,
    pierced the implacability, crying Lancelot, forgive me.

And so on – as I remarked. Do you not conceive that to be a

Percivale at Carbonek

very moving episode? Joy having to be forgiven for the necessity of its own birth?

As C. S. Lewis says: 'I do not know any other poet who could have conceived this scene'. It is central to Williams's thought, and the best commentary on it is his own essay on the Cross (*Image of the City*, p. 131).

1. Saffron sun: the Grail in Malory was heralded by a sunbeam of brightness seven times more than usual, and in Tennyson it was covered by a luminous cloud, but the saffron is, I think, C. W.'s own conception. See also 'The Coming of Galahad' and 'The Last Voyage', the pall that covers Blanchefleur.

9-10. Myrmidons: Achilles's followers, here Pelles's angelic household. Their beauty is 'unremitted' because not yet forgiven by fallen man; the word (now usually 'unremitting') also means 'constant'.

12. Even Galahad's unswerving purpose is checked by pity and grief.

16. Double misery: because the Table is destroyed and the Grail not won.

17 et seq. looks back to 'The Son of Lancelot'.

33. Engine: frozen in grief, Galahad's movements are mechanical?

34. Bors (in the poem as now developed) is to be the bearer because he is Lancelot's cousin, and because he represents the natural man who endures torment because of heavenly grace. The prayer and its answering forgiveness are made, as always, 'through another'.

39. The words of the General Thanksgiving in the Prayer Book. The necessity of being thankful is one of the hardest to accept.

Percivale at Carbonek

44. Bidding their birth: willing necessity.

47. In his footprints: grace submits to be led by common humanity to the climax of the Quest.

THE LAST VOYAGE

C. W.'s Note:
   The city and temple and Solomon were all painted on as if on a ship which was surrounded by dolphins. A remarkable picture, but possible.
   Hexameters and decasyllabics — both forms of the hazel, of 'measurement' in verse, categories of identity.
   'land melts': from the point of view of the lords, Logres is dissolving behind them (although Bors is to return); all that was Logres and the Empire has become this flight of doves driving the ship on its way; at the point where Galahad is so united with Christ that he has almost a necessity of being in himself; doctrinally heretical, I fear, but pass.
   'The hollow of Jerusalem' — the generative organs of this life are no more than the shoulder-hollows of Galahad. What *his* generative organs are, no-one has begun to imagine. He meets the Acts of the Emperor, and Byzantium and Sarras are in a sense one.

Further notes by A.M.H.

This poem and the next mark the end of Taliessin's story of the Grail in Logres, and of King Arthur and his knights and their experiences in establishing order in the country of Logres/Britain and seeking knowledge of the Grail. The story began at poem 3 in this book, 'The Vision of the Empire'.

1. The hollow of Jerusalem: the womb, holding present and future potentialities of people and civilisations. See 'The Vision of the Empire'. Also the map on the end papers of first edition of *Taliessin through Logres*.
   The poem is on three levels: of poetry; of exchange, substitution, and co-inherence discovered between man and God; of the Grail and King Arthur. There may be other levels for the reader to discover.

2. From here to l. 19 is description of world paintings in the hall of

The Last Voyage

the Emperor, presenting different means of power.

5. Dolphins: heraldic beast of Dinadan, the knight who was free from the ambitions and rivalries of the time.

13. Christians have the necessity of existence, i.e. redemption, in themselves through Christ. Achievement or agency, the purpose of the Empire drove on through distance, difficulty, enmity. The three knights (Galahad, Percival, Bors) who achieved the Grail, are on board.

34. Galahad the consecrated man, Percival the dedicated, Bors the married man in the life of the world. Poetry is part of the motion.

46. Infinite flight = all Logres and the Empire.

58-60. The approach of Aeneas's ship up the River Tiber where he founded the city of Rome. Cymodocea was a Nereid – water nymph.

63. The wonder that snapped: the fall of man, now redeemed.

65. Galahad, doing the work of steering the ship, was fulfilling a potentiality in man to reach perfection.

85-87. Gawaine: making peace with his doctrine became honour run mad. See 'Lamorack and the Queen Morgause of Orkney', line 44. Gawaine (legitimate) and Mordred the bastard destroyed the effort of the King and the Table.

101. See 'Percival at Carbonek', line 1.

106. Healing the wound of Pelles, and steering the ship.

116. Triangular speed equals fact, intelligence, flesh. See 'The Coming of Palomides'.

118. Necessity of being is God.

The Last Voyage

125. Ordinary Britain, but the ability for holiness remained within the kingdom centred in the castle of Carbonek. Which has recurred throughout history to the present day.

Logres, old name for the island of Britain, signified a place of holiness or some mystery, where the Holy Grail was lodged and spiritual beings brought awareness of the spiritual world. After the failure of Arthur, Carbonek remained a place and source of holiness, but the whole island was no longer called Logres but its geographical name of Britain, under the Roman Empire.

TALIESSIN AT LANCELOT'S MASS (A. R.)

The first version was printed in *New English Poetry*, 1931, and C.W. drew largely on it, in rhyme as well as in substance, for the later poem. The Malory reference is book XXI, chapters vii and x, though there Sir Bors is present in the flesh, and 'Sir Lancelot took the habit of priesthood of the Bishop, and a twelvemonth he sang mass'. It is a poem about reconciliation through substitution: Helayne for Guinevere, Pelles for Arthur; and Galahad stands for Christ in the substitution of the Mass.

2. See Malory, XXI.10.

10. The ritual takes place out of time. The 'white rushing deck' links it to the 'Last Voyage' and the Ship of Solomon.

13-20. Helayne became the mother of 'Logres' child' (Galahad) by substitution for Guinevere. See *Image of the City*, p. 177.

23. Garlon the invisible knight was brother to King Pelles and cause of the Dolorous Blow; see *Image of the City*, p. xxxvi. In his Notes which are printed there, C. W. wrote: 'Garlon . . is Satan to us but the Holy Ghost to the supernatural powers'.

30. Attributed: see 'The Parable of the Wedding Garment'. (*Image of the City*, p. 166)

33. Epiclesis: invoking the Holy Spirit.

36. Theotokos: the Mother of God.

40. Acts: see 'The Vision of the Empire'.

42. Gyre: perhaps a reminiscence of Yeats's 'Sailing to Byzantium', 'Come from the holy fire, pern in a gyre'.

48. The porphyry stair gave access to the Emperor, but also stands for the gate of birth.

Taliessin at Lancelot's Mass

51. Web of co-inherence, as in line 21.

56. The dismissal in the Latin Mass.

57. I once referred to C. W.'s Order as his 'salvaged household', and the word became a favourite with him.

The end of the poem returns us to history. Logres becomes the historical Britain (see the previous poem), and the Taliessin of the myth returns as it were to private life.

POEMS FROM THE REGION OF THE SUMMER STARS

(Poetry London, 1944)

Title: The phrase comes from a poem by the poet Taliesin (*sic*) in the *Mabinogion*, a collection of Welsh tales compiled in the 14th and 15th centuries, and published in her English translation by Lady Charlotte Guest in 1849. Tennyson in the *Idylls of the King* made Taliessin (adding the extra s) the chief poet at King Arthur's court.

PREFACE (T. S.)

The poet introduces his new poems as generally incidental to the main theme of *Taliessin through Logres* (OUP 1938), the argument of which he here summarises. It may seem to be, in fact, an expansion and elucidation of the way of life through the method of exchange and substitution, as posited in the Christian faith.

PRELUDE (T. S.)

Conceptions of civilised man, society, Greek philosophy, Roman Government, Jewish religion – infiltrated by the Christian dogma of the Incarnation, shown to fulfil them all.

1. Irony: capable of many interpretations and contradictions and coincidences.

10. Bible: *Acts of Apostles* XVII.23.

12. Bible: St. Paul's second epistle to *Corinthians* XII.7.

13-14. E.g., He saved others, himself he could not save.

15. Gold: symbolic colour of perfection.
   Ambiguity: doubtful or double meaning, integration of God with man, flesh with Spirit. 'This also is thou; neither is This thou' (Intro. *Descent of the Dove*).

RSS: Prelude

16-18. Creature: man seen as created.
Vocabulary of faith, etc. In Bible, *New Testament*, St. Paul's Epistles.

19. Handfasted, betrothed, espoused.

23. Main: as in Might and – utmost strength. (*Descent of the Dove*, pages 12-14)

25. Leaders in that heresy which limits salvation to only part of creation.

26. Careful: Nestorius was a leading teacher of the doctrine that there were in Christ two beings united by a moral union and not one divine person.
The body and the physical creation are not included in redemption and eternal life (C. W. *Descent of the Dove*, p. 70).

30. Theotokos: Mother of God. Anthropotokos: Mother of Man.

31-36. Bloodshed convinced Nestorians that 'Moral union' was a less dangerous proposition than coinherence.

37-41. Emperor moves his organisation, secular and ecclesiastic, to Byzantium. Local Christians remain in Rome under the priest who came to be called the Pope.

41. Manumission: setting free from slavery. Jews and Romans usually freed a slave after 7 years.

44-46. Bible, *Revelation*, I.9-18.

53-55. E.g. SS Anthony, Basil; Princess Dindrane; Taliessin.

56. The Pope, in white robes in the church of St. John Lateran, like the spirit of a man awaiting his physical body.

61. Grail...Deivirilis: C. W.'s *Descent of the Dove*, pp. 115-17: 'He (Galahad; man achieving Grail) is flesh and blood in the union with the Flesh and the Blood'.

62. Singly borne in Grail.

63. 'The Doctrine of the Holy Trinity is wholly practical' et seq. (*New Christian Year*, passage for Trinity Monday. Law, An Appeal. 'To Michal: On Bringing Her Breakfast in Bed', *Windows of Night.*) Visionary hierarchy at work in celestial city; as in heaven, so on earth.

74. In hell, exchange is repudiated.

84. P'o-l'u: see 'Vision of the Empire', 'Prayers of the Pope'.

92-96. See *Arthurian Torso*, p. 70.

97. Priest and victim: coinherence.

97-99. C. W. 1940: 'I send you a poem which I have written ('Taliessin in the Rose Garden') . . . it is obscure, but you may recognise some ideas: the blood of war, of women, of Jesus'.

THE CALLING OF TALIESSIN
(J.W., A.R., A.M.H., AND A.S.)

Letter of 27 May 1943: 'I have sent eight poems to this fellow [i.e. Tambimuttu] who wants to do a pamphlet', and letter of 20 August 1943: 'I wait – with slight impatience – for the proofs of the eight poems which are to make up the *Region of the Summer Stars*, there are some good things in it'.

The first 7 lines of the *Book of Taliesin* speculate on lineage, but 'none knew; no clue he showed...'. The origin of the Grail story can look to Celtic, Classical, or Christian sources. Charles held them all in mind, but his own poems rise more from Malory than from the Welsh myths. In conversation he saw himself as a poet creating Taliessin the poet by way of Milton, and Tennyson and Swinburne.

IV:
3. Taliessin heard a word of the Empire; he heard / tales of the tree of Adam: this was the call to Taliessin, the search for the City 'of the Sacred Emperor at operative Byzantium'. The 'poor, goetic or theurgic, the former spells' are black and natural forms of magic, now seen as poor, inadequate against the 'moulded themes of the Empire'.

VI:
1 et seq. Here C. W. amplifies our knowledge of the sea-wood Broceliande, the place of making, already touched on in these Notes. Those who study the 'matter of the marches', parts of Empire remote from the central intellect, know that there the divine science (mathematics and philosophy) and the grand art (poetry) meet and affect each other. The third heaven is the sphere of Venus, divine love, of which earthly love is the reflection, and it is the sphere of Nimue, mistress of Broceliande, mother of Merlin and Brisen; we see in her 'all the vast processes of the universe imaged in a single figure' (*Figure of Arthur*, p. 82).

For some who enter the sea-wood, the vision is too overwhelming, they emerge 'gustily audacious' because it has

The Calling of Taliessin

overthrown control.

10. By currying horses: a curry-comb is used to comb down or groom horses.

VII:

1. ...yet unmade Logres: Arthur and the Order are not yet established.

5. Dark rose of sunset: a significant colour for Williams; here and at line 148 it is the antipodean opposite of the 'dark-rose, self-glowing' point of the Trinity later in the poem.

7-11. P'o-l'u is visible beyond Broceliande, and at the sight of it the poet dreads that he might betray his art, losing proper attention to reality (the sense of identity and difference), no longer acquitted of his shortcomings for the sake of his skill, 'a thrilling rhyme'.

16. From the *Book of Taliesin* in the *Mabinogion* (pp. 273-74 in Everyman edition).

21. Wood of suicides: see the *Inferno*, Canto 12.

VIII, IX:
13 et seq.; 1 et seq. Taliessin in his fear and desolation is in need of succour, and so invokes Mary Magdalene 'who had charity for Christ'. (Perhaps there is some further significance here which I have missed.) Merlin and Brisen stand for Time and Space, masculine and feminine, and are ultimately one being. They are black-haired – Merlin is *young* in Williams's conception of the myth, and in *The Figure of Arthur* he credits Geoffrey of Monmouth with the invention of the sage as a young man (p. 33). They were born by parthenogenesis of Nimue in Broceliande, and sent by her to establish Arthur's court at Camelot, the equivalent of Pelles's kingdom at Carbonek where the Grail is.

IX:
24. His daughter: Helayne, who is to be the mother of Galahad.

The Calling of Taliessin

X:
15. The time has come for the Grail to appear openly in Logres and be known in man's outward life.

XI:
8. Stones of the waste: those who seem to be failures.

26. Magical continuum: a series of elements passing into each other.

XIII:
2. The porphyry stair in the Emperor's palace in Byzantium, which led from the entrance hall to the throne room, was always a central image in C. W.'s verse: see 'The Vision of Empire' and especially 'Taliessin in the School of the Poets'. Porphyry is a very hard and beautiful, dark crimson or purple rock.

13. The imagery of the crowns and choirs is taken (like that in 'Mount Badon') from the Book of Revelation. See also the final canto of Dante's *Paradiso*.

XIV:
5. Taliessin sees in his vision what ought to have come to pass in Logres, had not sin (as instanced by Arthur's self-love and incest, Guinevere and Lancelot's adulterous love, Balin's blind murderous rage, and Mordred's envy and greed and resentment) prevented the fulfilment of the original purpose. He sees Logres unified in Brisen's shadow from its base in the potentialities of Broceliande to its fully conscious reason and will in the court of Arthur at the summit, all 'waiting and watching' for the imminent revelation of the divine presence.

33. Taliessin sees a princess holding the Grail, who might be (a) someone whom even to look at was 'more than his function' (ll. 357-61), or (b) Nimue (ll. 362-64), or (c) Dindrane (ll. 364-68), or (d) Helayne. Who is (a)? I think that here we have the last — and in the later poems the only — appearance of the Princess of

The Calling of Taliessin

Byzantium who figures in the early Arthurian poems. In his book of *Three Plays*, published in 1931, the plays are set between four Arthurian poems, of which the second is called 'Taliessin's Song of Byzantion' and contains the stanzas:

> In the gate of Saint Sophia I saw a princess stand
> clad all in golden burnished robes, on the Emperor's right hand;
> with clasped and hieratic hands among the strings and swords
> A princess of Byzantion looked forth above the lords...
>
> But within the Holy Wisdom, where the popes and patriarchs were,
> ere I turned to leave Byzantion I louted low to her
> where her face looked forth beyond me, in her Father's glory dim,
> as in galaxies of splendour from the wings of seraphim.

50. These lines recall the seventh stanza of 'Taliessin at Lancelot's Mass' and the poem 'The Founding of the Company' which also deal with the household of Taliessin.

TALIESSIN IN THE ROSE-GARDEN (T. S.)

See Note to *R.S.S.* 'Prelude', lines 97-99.
Anne Scott, a friend of Charles's, at hand when the poem was written, has kindly shared with me their discussions on the subject. The poem is another moment of truth, caught in the simultaneity of Time.

Ideas recognised:
  a. 'Who can find a virtuous woman? For her price is far above rubies.' (*Proverbs* XXXI.10)
  b. Discipline: self-discipline: being adult in love: 'But where a child submits, an adult freely submits; the difference is not negligible. Authority does not, among the adult, do away with freedom; freedom indeed lies precisely in the choice of submission'. (*Flecker of Dean Close*, pp. 80-81 et seq. C. W.)
  c. Coherence of body and spirit: i.e. Everyman and woman, seen in the Adam as one body, co-inhering in the mind of God, whose idea it was anyway. (Postscript: *Descent of the Dove*, C.W.). Separation of body and spirit causing incoherence, shown in physical and mental dis-ease, and the overthrowing of balance and justice in temporal government.
  d. Coherence in healthy circulation of blood in the body, with monthly damming and discharge in the mature woman, in readiness for possible conception of offspring. Connection herein between Everywoman and Mary, Mother of God, with the shedding of the blood of her son Jesus for the salvation of mankind; with the showing of reconciliation in the co-inherence with the Holy Trinity, as constantly recollected in the image of the Eucharist.

I:
1 et seq. Implies the necessity of discipline and rule in the natural growth and function for fertility and fruition, whether in queens, roses, poetry.

2. See stanza IV, lines 18-19.

6. Among the earliest known roses; still in rose catalogues – Rosa

Taliessin in the Rose-Garden

Centifolia – hundred-petalled.

12. Implicit: Holy Trinity.

14-16. Explicit: i. Woman in command (affirmation of images)
  ii. Woman dedicated to God (rejection of images)
  iii. Woman in the street.
Each subject to the laws of nature and rules of the city.

15. Percivale: contemplative, with Galahad and Bors achieved the Grail.

18. Eidolon: image of one submissively devoted – a slave.

II:
1-5. Nature's beauty, setting for physical beauty of Queen. Unlike the heavenly planet, earth is at the mercy of Broceliande (Nimue's place of making and breaking) and its constant movement in being.

6. Acute physical awareness unusual for Taliessin: heightened consciousness opens his eyes, so he sees in the ruby, as Merlin in his magical crystal, (ll. 19-20) what will happen to Logres-in-the-Empire – because (l. 31) of the Queen's failure as example of perfect Womanhood.

33. Image of the wounding of Christ – though in Pelles it was due to contingency of hallowed spear and fighting – furious Balin.

III:
Instead, now, of seeing 'how the City was based, faced fair to the Emperor as the queen to the king, slaves to lords, and all Caucasia to Carbonek' (IV, l. 8).

5. Taliessin sees Guinevere looking askance for Lancelot.

6. He recalls other unsuccessful lovers – Palomides; himself.

Taliessin in the Rose-Garden

8. True, Taliessin desires the beloved in the fashion of the mythical unicorn, an 'alien love', its consummation in 'intellectual nuptials unclosed'. (See 'Taliessin's Song of the Unicorn', *TTL*). This arch-natural attitude, natural man finds (l. 9) un-natural; natural woman, merely silly.

10. Hint: of perfection. Palomides, sharing the poetical experience, cannot – will not – be reconciled to contemplating the image of God, in the unattainable Beloved. The Palomides poems in *TTL* tell of his frustrations, humiliations, and shame.

17. Shent: past tense and past participle of shend (obs. or poet.): to put to shame, to disgrace, reproach, punish, discomfit. P. intended to do great things, including healing the wounded King.

10-17. Bitter brew of exchange: after labouring to build one's altar, the heavenly fire comes down on another's. (See VI, 11-15; The Bible, *Genesis* Ch. V.)

IV:
1. The Jews find this unfair, so unworthy of God; as is his degrading death: scandalous. The Greeks, disdaining the building of altars anyway, find a God who lets himself be killed is foolish indeed.

2. Taliessin, brought up in the earthly religion of the Druids, coming to be educated in Byzantium, his (l. 6) mind on the substantial being of Logres, finds a (l. 7) new myth in the spiritual talk of the prelates, and (l. 11) magnanimity of the Emperor's court.

11. Stair: transposed epithet for Emperor.

13-19. Taliessin finds contemporary myth of Zodiac a convenient image of the Co-inherence of the Universe. The sun makes an annual journey around the earth and other planets (as the blood circulates through veins, arteries, organs of the human body) passing in seasonal order through the Houses (lunar months), the qualities of which are supposed, in Astrology, to influence the

Taliessin in the Rose-Garden

affairs of human beings born under their signs. The myth gives scope for contingent disasters inherent in the vagaries of natural phenomena in the universe and in mankind, and points the indissoluble relationship of each to all.

18-19. See stanza I, line 2. Man works according to his own character and capacity; ideally, for the well-being of the community.

In the *Taliessin through Logres* end-paper map of the Empire, with superimposed female figure, the four Houses Taliessin chooses, as germane to (l. 20) his purpose, would show Aquarius, eyes, the principle of seeing, in the head, over Logres.

29. Gemini, the twins, in the hands, used in labour and blessing, at Rome, which had been built by the fabled twins Romulus and Remus and which became the seat of the Pope, the head of the Christian Church, Vice-regent on earth of God.

34. Libra, principle of balance and justice is well set in Caucasia, the stable foundation and rich bottom of the Empire.

37. Scorpio, the fully armed and armoured creature, with its reflex action to danger, is the image of contingency – the unforeseen occurrence which causes a sword to flash, or a button to be pushed, and so looses catastrophe upon the world. In the map, Scorpio straddles the meeting-place of flesh and spirit in exchange and substitution for mankind, the genitalia; at Jerusalem the acknowledged holiest place of worshipful exchange between man and God. It is worth noting that there are no contingencies in the life on earth of the Son of God.

39. As flesh to Spirit; as mankind to the Land of the Trinity.

V:
1-12. An illustration from a medieval Book of Hours expressed in poetry, as Taliessin visualises the Queen and Logres as it could have been.

Taliessin in the Rose-Garden

18. Equality between man and woman lies precisely in their difference fitting into one-ness — being at-oned; in willing submission to the facts of the inherent design — Caucasia and the City in fair conjunction.

23-24. Scandal or folly, all reconciled in poetry.

VI sees the reverse of IV:
1. Arch-natural justice: as unacceptable to mankind as arch-natural love (stanza III.8-9).

7. The mystery of the Christian myth is almost impossible for mankind, whose natural reaction to the unknown, i.e. fear, is physical violence. 'We are slayers all, from our mothers' wombs'. (Letter from C. W.)

32-33. Flesh, in the instant, refuses to know what spirit knows, and so we have constantly, 'heaven ruining from heaven' (Milton, *Paradise Lost*).

VI:
11-15. See *Genesis* V. Murder is outrage, in the organic, as in the politic body.

17. Rome built, Romulus murders Remus.

20. Taliessin climbs through everything falling.

21. Light: of Transfiguration: of Salvation.

25-26. As if looking at the end-paper map.

27. Again, Bible reference to the story of the Fall.

28. Atonement: at-one-ment in the mystery of the substitution of Christ's blood in the Chalice, in the sacrament of the Eucharist.

29. N.B. to warn is not to forbid, but to bid take care to understand

Taliessin in the Rose-Garden

fully what is being undertaken.

30. Christ is victim and priest. Woman is victim (l. 31) and mother of victim.

32. Mother-wit (flesh) knows what wisdom (spirit) (l. 33) knows: wisdom understands (l. 34) the facts of Womanhood's physical life can be seen in the myth; in her willing submission to it.

37. Guinevere's failure lies in her – unwittingness? unwillingness? – inability in some sort, to come to terms with reality: to reconcile Caucasia with Carbonek, to come to maturity in Camelot; to give herself to the journey, in fact.

VII:
A glorious paean in praise of Womankind in her relationship to the Christian myth.

2. Travel and travail.

4. Anthropometry: comparative study of sizes and proportion of the human body.

6. Jupiter, a Zodiac planet with Saturn, Venus, Earth, Mars, and Mercury. Reference to convenient great Red Spot remarked in 1878, but probably earlier.

5-15. Taunt: Himself he could not save; truth: Christ saves Mankind in Himself, and so himself. No irony. (See also last lines of 'Coming of Galahad', *TTL*.)

20-21. Image of exchange and substitution, and reconciliation in 'This also is Thou: neither is this Thou'.
    'His honour rooted in dishonour stood,
   And faith unfaithful kept him falsely true'.
      (Tennyson: 'Lancelot and Elaine')

DEPARTURE OF DINDRANE (J. W.)

In the 'Calling of Taliessin', Dindrane appears as the sister of Percivale (ll. 376-78):
> she who was called Blanchfleur in religion, and to be
> farther from and closer to the king's poet
> than any,...

In 'The Departure of Dindrane' the household of Taliessin waits in the courtyard for 'the two lords'.

II:
10. *Logres kept the old Levitical law*: Chrétien de Troyes wrote four poems and in one of them, 'Lancelot', is found the first definition of Logres as the land of King Arthur (from Welsh Lloegr or land of King Arthur, which was also Britain or within Britain), page 53, *Arthurian Torso*, Charles Williams and C. S. Lewis.

III:
4. *Now near freedom, she brooded on choice* –: The second theme of the poem is announced, the choice to be made by the slave girl and the 'Departure' is described by her, and coloured by reflections on her own situation.

V:
17. *The hazel of the cattle-goad, of the measuring rod*: is also Dindrane's bare arm. In 'The Making of Taliessin' (*The Image of the City*, p. 182) Charles wrote, 'It occurred to me that in the traditions this rod was normally of hazel, and the dictionary confirmed this'.

29. *Servitude and freedom were one and interchangeable*: a key line, Blanchefleur rides to her vocation, Taliessin will accompany her from the City.

VI:
4 et seq. *'I will ride through the suburbs beside you'* towards 'the convent of Almesbury': they will part, in love, and to the slave girl the 'lords' covered against the rain are 'two centaur shapes, cloaked

to the haunches'. The centauri were originally bull-killers. In later Greek accounts they were represented as half-man, half-horse. This is how a mounted Spaniard was regarded by the native Americans. To the slave girl her 'lords' at that moment were more than human beings.

VII:
10 et seq. She heard in the air, above the centaurs, a voice / drop from the third heaven – fixed is the full: In the rain-drenched world of the journey the future is glimpsed of 'the foster-ward' of Dindrane before his birth'.

21. The grand Rejection sang to the grand Affirmation: Without the act of Dindrane there could be no future salutation from Galahad to his 'my lord, Sir Lancelot my father'.

VIII:
1 et seq. As a halt is called, 'Untie! Untie! the two-handed shape disbanded before her'. Farewells are said, the travellers leave in opposite directions.

31. Seven days afterwards, before the king's bailiff: the slave girl chooses that her fortune should be in the household of her lord Taliessin.

Letter of 20 August 1943: 'I can see dimly in the distance the point at which Taliessin is no longer enough, and We proceed to Percivale'.

THE FOUNDING OF THE COMPANY (A. R.)

At the beginning of the Second World War, C.W. sent to some of his friends a draft Promulgation of the Order of the Co-inherence, 'dated as from the Feast of the Annunciation; it is proposed that the formal foundation (in so far as this can be) shall be recognised as from the Feast of Trinity next'. He invited comments on the draft, which was being sent only to those already acquainted with the principle embodied in the Order, and added that the final plan should be submitted if possible to episcopal consideration.

There are seven items in the draft, the first of which says that: 'The Order has no constitution except in its members', and the second 'It recommends nevertheless that its members shall make a formal act of union with it and of recognition of their own nature'. The third defines its concern as 'the practice of the apprehension of the Co-inherence both as a natural and supernatural principle'. Three further paragraphs amplify this, and item 7 recommends that the Order is to be associated primarily with four feasts: the Annunciation, Trinity, Transfiguration, and All Souls.

The mythical figures of C. W.'s imagination were created, as we know, from the characters and places of his actual life. The Company described in the poem bears the same relation to this Order as does the 'king's poet' to Charles himself, or, say, the City of God to its exemplar in Amen House. In the human as in the mythical Order, there was 'no vote or admission, / but for the single note that any soul / took of its own election of the Way'; the concern of both is the co-inherence of all souls with each other and with God.

I:
2-3. Tabennisi: St. Pachomius founded in 320 at Tabennisi, near the Nile, the first 'coenobitic' (i.e. living in common) monastery, whose Rule influenced St. Basil. The three 'Cappadocian Fathers' were St. Basil, his brother St. Gregory of Nyssa, and St. Gregory of Nazianzus.

    Monte Cassino: the monastery founded by St. Benedict in 529.

The Founding of the Company

13. Pacts of the themes: different parts of the Empire, pledged to its service.

23. *Quicunque vult*: from the Athanasian Creed, often quoted by C. W. 'Whosoever will be saved, before all things it is necessary that he hold the Catholic Faith . . . and the Catholic Faith is this: That we worship one God in Trinity, and Trinity in Unity'.

25. Doctrine of largesse: the giving that asks no return, and is quite independent of desert.

27. Mansion: dwelling-place.

II:
1-7. The Companions are spread over the whole Empire, in its form like the human body.

10 et seq. The hazel as always stands for measurement, whether in verse or mathematics. The poem distinguishes three 'stations' or modes of being, none being greater or less than another. The first is the ordinary exchange of human living, which is only repudiated in hell – P'o-l'u – where each would live for himself.

III:
The second 'mode' is the mystical exchange, of which the supreme example is the sacrifice for man, which is practised by contemplatives when they partake in imagination of Christ's sufferings, and which now the Company try to practise in bearing each other's burdens. See 'Bors to Elayne' (in *Taliessin through Logres*): What saith Heracleitus? – and what is the City's breath? – *dying each other's life; living each other's death.*

IV:
The third mode images that of the Trinity itself, supreme type of co-inherence. Mary partook of that nature, when Christ whom she bore took flesh from her.

The Founding of the Company

12. See 'The Calling of Taliessin', in which the king's poet had a vision of the land of the Trinity, which is Sarras, where Bors, Percivale, and Galahad will arrive at the end of the quest, 'among moving rocks and granite voices' ('Prayers of the Pope').

24. Perichoresis, or circumincession, is the theological term for the interpenetration of the Persons of the Trinity.

V:
1. The Feast of All Fools, April 1, and specially appropriate to the irony of Dinadan, is when the lowest is called greatest.

3. Belated verse: too many things have distracted the poet from the work he was born to do; in this discouraged mood Taliessin and C.W. are one. As also in 13-14; of St. Paul: 'Lest when I have preached to others, I myself should be a castaway' (1 *Cor*. IX.25).

17. Dinadan reminds him that he is to be saved by others, superfluous, even when he was leader.

30. This is a variant on a favourite exhortation of C.W.'s: 'St. Thomas! and charge, Zion!'

43. The doctrine of largesse: none can earn it, freely given, freely received.

VI:
The King's poet is acknowledged by the Company as their head, but only in a heavenly mockery, for none is greater than another.

11. Christ-taunting: 'He saved others, himself he cannot save' (*Matt*. XXVII.42).

THE QUEEN'S SERVANT (A.M.H.)

A letter of C. W. to me in 1939, war time, shows he was working on these Summer Stars poems in a group. He was thinking of the whole population of Logres, its social order and groups of the people high and low, and their interlocking responsibilities and skills.

1-10. Sir Kay at the King's Court wrote to Taliessin for a recommendation of a maid to work for the Queen in the palace at Camelot, one who could read Greek, superintend laying out a rose-garden, wait on the Queen in her official work and in official ceremonies and have some knowledge of poetry 'the grand art'.

11 et seq. Taliessin knows his staff well. He had formerly bought a slave and found her skilful and ready to learn. Now he sends for her and says he will equip her for the task. They talk of the project, and of her past life.

37 et seq. Taliessin tells the slave girl to throw off her clothes. He sees that her fair body is matched by a fair soul. Here was a glimpse of a natural blooming and fructiferous life, which is known in different levels in the provinces of Broceliande and Caucasia and in Camelot, man's nature growing under the Creator's hand, and even shared by the Creator in the child and young man Jesus.

40. Sarras is the heavenly city of the spiritual life, known in timeless moments by some living people, and to which the blessed dead from our earth go.

48-95. Taliessin by a sweet skill of music and movement filled the room with roses round the once-slave girl. The roses changed to make a crimson gown and cloak. He put on the girl his own brooch, new shoes, and her old slave's belt
      for a bond and a quiet oath
   to gather freedom as once she gathered servitude.

102 et seq. She asked for some token which was a gift between Taliessin her old master and herself, and was not part of the Rite of freedom she had just gone through. He understood. She was to live now a whole person, undivided by slave's status. Lightly he struck her face for the gift, as in slavery her body might be beaten by another's choice for punishment or cruelty. Immediately, she knew she was wholly free, a woman redeemed by Christ and a citizen of Logres like Taliessin.

THE MEDITATION OF MORDRED (A. S.)

Mordred's meditation displays him as wholly self-enclosed, self-centred, and self-interested, despising everyone else, a million miles from any conception of comradeship or co-inherence.

1-2. The Pope has written to Arthur bidding him be reconciled with Lancelot. The King has torn up the letters in a rage and crossed the Channel with his army to besiege Lancelot in his castle in Berwick

9. I rest on his palace roof: In 'Bors to Elayne: On the King's Coins', *Taliessin through Logres*, Bors 'saw the dragonlets' eyes / Leer and peer, and the house-roofs under their weight / Creak and break'. Now Mordred sees himself as a dragon stretched out on the palace roof waiting for his moment.

11. My uncanonical father: Uncanonical is the ecclesiastical equivalent of illegitimate. Mordred's birth was the result of an act of adultery and incest which broke the canon law of the Church.

19. Laidly: = loathly.
    Wittol: = an acquiescent cuckold.

31. Adsum: = I am present; here I am. It used to be the word with which schoolboys answered to their name at roll-call.

33. The nit-witted wittols of worldly wisdom: As the wittol acquiesces in the sin of his wife, so the citizens acquiesce in the sin of the king in withholding the tribute due to the Emperor in Byzantium.

37-42. The sacredness of the Grail means nothing to Mordred. *If* it exists he sees it as a luck-charm, a piece of 'fairy mechanism' which might give magical assistance to his cooks.

48. I am indebted to Mr Richard Jeffery for discovering Zemarchus in the 11th edition of the *Encyclopaedia Britannica*. In 568 he led a Byzantine embassy to confirm an alliance and a silk-trade

The Meditation of Mordred

treaty with a Turkish khan in Central Asia. C. W. evidently borrowed the name and the connection with trade and travel from this story.

68. Mordred's ideal – 'alone' – is the negation of all co-inherence.

THE PRAYERS OF THE POPE
(T. S. & J. W.)

It was all prefigured in the compression of 'The Prelude' to *Taliessin through Logres*; manifested in the characters and their stories throughout that volume, and in the subsequent *Region of the Summer Stars* (to which Charles himself wrote an illuminating preface), and brought to its full revelation in this concluding poem, as C. S. Lewis had surmised that it would be (*Arthurian Torso*, page 95). Anne Ridler writes: '...in the Prayers of the Pope (the last of the poems we have) there is a drawing together of the separate events: we are given not the *why* but the *how* of the schism and the redemption . . . the Pope (rich in *voluntary* loss) celebrates the Christmas Eucharist, and in that action takes upon himself the heartbreak of the division in Man, in the Kingdom, in the World' (*Image of the City*, Intro., p. lxv).

N.B. It is a good idea to keep the end-paper map handy. The well-being of the Empire and of each individual in the Empire, are interdependent.

I:

2. Pope Adeodatus ?AD 672-76 (*Chambers Encyclopaedia*). Egyptian-born, to remind us that the Roman Church may have 'seized, as by a creative intuition, on the idea of Order as the basis of the universe . . . But the spiritual presentation of the theory came not from Europe, but from Africa...'? (C. W. quotes, in *The Descent of the Dove*, p. 98, from Cruttwell's *Literary History of the Early Church*.)

4-7. Reference to hypnotic trance of Nimue's twins, Merlin and Brisen — Time and Space — in 'Calling of Taliessin' (Para. IX).

5. Civilised *human* being (the Adam, inherent male and female principles) in measured time, defined space, linking nature and super-nature, flesh, and spirit.

6. 'And do you think the Pope, who is young, with white hair, brilliant, the image of Merlin (only Merlin has black hair), might be

The Prayers of the Pope

Merlin + loss? If you get me. The Pope (let us say) is time losing its beauties (by deprivation or will, not by mere passing change) but affirmatively...'. (Letter to Anne Ridler in answer to her plea that Charles should print such elucidations of puzzling passages.)

9. Eastern Church's mode of administering Communion – consecrated wafer dipped in wine, dried; kept for adoration, and ministering to the sick or dying.

10. Three Christmas Masses: 1. Midnight, 2. Dawn, 3. Mass of the day.

12-15. Integration of Classical Latin – official language of Roman government, literature, religion – with Italian vernacular: involvement of ancient gods and customs with Christianity – e.g. Lupercal, the feast of Lupercus god of fertility and flocks, and Lateran (see line 2), pertaining to the Pope's Cathedral Church, founded on the site of pre-Christian basilica.

14. Genesis: beginning – Christ-child's Birthday.

15. Quickening: becoming alive – in fact and in verse – movement of flesh and spirit into soul.

16. Pontiff: bridge-builder, accepted means of communication between sons of men and Son of God.
   Magnificat (St. Luke's Gospel, I.46-55): Virgin Mary's thanksgiving that the Son of God is to be in her as the Son of Man. The riches of which she sings, beggar those who lose worldly possessions.

17. Meditating thus, the Pope is caught up in the thought of the loss of this Beloved, death implicit in birth, as in all mankind; but this, God Himself, the image of man, and yet a man; dying to save mankind.

21-23. '...each remembered his singular particular loss. The king felt: "Now the dynasty fails". Bors felt: "Farms and manors are burned, the corn lost, the poor returned to starvation...". Lancelot felt: "If we win, after this, her kiss is the king's...". Only Taliessin, in the west with the king, smiled to think how the household had founded a new Order...' (lines from early version of poem 'Divites Dimisit, for Michal in memory of the darkness 1914-17').

25. The Pope realises that more wealth lies in the loss of having than in the keeping, and with a new twist prays that we, the rich, may not be sent empty away.

II:
A moment of co-inherence had been envisaged when 'the glory of the Emperor stretched to the ends of the world' (Part I, 'Prelude', *T.T.L.*) but as in the earlier poem, 'the chosen champions of the Empire forgot the Empire'.

1-9. The Pope broods on the manner of it — 'not the *why* but the *how*' — with each governor of each province seeing himself as potential operative Providence, and dissociating himself from the Imperial vision, ignoring the ignorant invaders.

20. Necromancy: art of revealing the future by communication with spirits of the dead.
   Gnosis: each gnostic sect, flourishing among early Christians, 'professed a gnosis or assured revelation on the nature of God, on his intermediaries to the world, and on the possibility of salvation from evil...' (*Chambers Encyclopaedia*).

III:
1. *Substance* of image and loss reiterated cf. Para. I, line 9.

2. Blessed in the loss of the body of the Son of Man.

6. Double instead of single image, for flesh and spirit are at variance.

8. The Son of God having been, in the Son of Man, the loss itself, bears also the image of the loss.

The Prayers of the Pope

IV:
1-5. From the particular wars engendered in Para. II, the Pope apprehends the beginnings of all wars. Citizens pressed to the defence of civilised living in London, Paris (Lutetia – its Roman name), or wherever, by their governors whose word is law.

V:
The only difference between us and the enemy lies in our knowledge that there is none. We know what we think we are doing, but not how they think. We know that if we are to be forgiven, we must forgive – and being forgiven is the difficulty. Affirming and denying, we can intend repentance both ways, if we are reconciled to loss as wealth.

VI:
In Para. IV, the Pope saw physical force pursuing vengeance to the death. Now he opens his mind to 'treachery, to tyranny, to all lust of self' (unpublished sonnet 1929) in which evil becomes the objective. 'Evil be thou my good' says Lucifer in *Paradise Lost*. The mind of man plumbs the depths of depravity in deliberate violation of all sanctity.

30-34. Even the most civilised hardly blench at the excesses of war.

VII:
Through the particular, Para. II, to the general, IV, to the cataclysmic, VI, we have come full circle from Para. I; from the personal image of the Son of God, becoming the Son of Man, for the salvation of man, to the image of that man in the person of the Pope: the organic body of mankind, image of the organic body of the Empire, each in all, all in each. (See *T.T.L.* end-papers map.)

He feels the dereliction of the Empire in his own being – dissolution of body and soul. Divisions in the flesh by cancers and tumours; the good of intellect lost in transgression; virtue and grace claimed as compensation for the breakdown of his integrity by his own sins.

The Prayers of the Pope

11 et seq. Category: umbrella term for arbitrary collection of individuals, identifiable only by initial, age, race, colour, religion, occupation . . . therefore without identity. Glory of Empire lies in the identification of each entity with others and all with it in co-inherence.

By 324 the Roman Emperor Constantine had united the East and West sections of the Empire, and by 326 the city of Byzantium became the official capital and renamed Constantinople. The Emperor had summoned Bishops to a Council in 325, so had been active in promoting the creation of true doctrine.

VIII:
It is now a time of crises, 'the indivisible Empire was divided' and the poem alternates between the prayers of the Pope and the action of Taliessin in dissolving the outer structure of the Company/Household. Mordred has divided Logres in his rebellion against his father King Arthur. Logres is a province of the Empire with its centre at Byzantium. It has been suggested that until the 5th century Christianity as practised in Roman Britain was closer to Byzantine practices than to Roman. But how does this line up with the dates of the Pope?

XIII:
With the breaking up of the 'bounds of the Empire' the giant octopods move beyond P'o-l'u to menace 'along Burma, nearing India' (see end-map of *Taliessin through Logres*). But the roots of Broceliande fasten on the octopods, they are 'hanging helpless' and the headless Emperor sinks as a crimson stain into the ocean. It is the opposite image of the roses in the gardens of Caucasia.

54 et seq. Life in the Empire is renewed, 'the lords stirred', roses bloom again and 'the women of Burma walked with the women of Caerleon'.

XIV-XV:
This followed, and the poem ends by the Pope's prayer in which he uses the particularly Byzantine image of the Harrowing of Hell. In

The Prayers of the Pope

his singing of the 'Christmas Eucharist' prayers are offered for 'the bodies and souls of the dead' as he offers 'his soul's health for the living corpses'. Kneeling after the Eucharist the Pope's last prayer echoes an earlier one 'Send not, send not, the rich empty away'.

www.ingramcontent.com/pod-product-compliance
Lightning Source LLC
Chambersburg PA
CBHW030003050426
42451CB00006B/93